New Jersey School Law

New Jersey School Law

With Notes, Blanks and Forms

New Jersey School Law

New Jersey School Law
With Notes, Blanks and Forms

ISBN/EAN: 9783337232498

Printed in Europe, USA, Canada, Australia, Japan

Cover: Foto ©Suzi / pixelio.de

More available books at **www.hansebooks.com**

NEW JERSEY SCHOOL LAW,

WITH

Notes, Blanks and Forms

FOR THE USE AND GOVERNMENT OF

SCHOOL OFFICERS,

PREPARED BY THE

State Superintendent of Public Instruction.

To be Preserved and Delivered by Each Officer to His Successor.

TRENTON, N. J.:
JOHN L. MURPHY, BOOK AND JOB PRINTER.

1881.

THE SCHOOL LAW.

REVISION—1874, WITH AMENDMENTS.

An Act to Establish a System of Public Instruction.

A.—STATE BOARD OF EDUCATION.

1. BE IT ENACTED *by the Senate and General Assembly of the State of New Jersey*, That the general supervision and control of public instruction in the State of New Jersey shall be vested in a state board of education, which board shall consist of the trustees of the school fund, the trustees of the state normal school, appointed as hereafter provided, together with the treasurer thereof. **State Board, how composed.**

1*a*. A quorum of the state board of education shall consist of eight members.* **Quorum.**

2. The state board of education shall have power, and it shall be their duty: **Powers and duties.**

I. To frame and modify at pleasure such by-laws as may be deemed expedient for their own government, not inconsistent with the provisions of this act, and to prescribe and cause to be enforced all rules and regulations necessary for carrying into effect the school laws of this state;

II. To consider the necessities of the public schools, and recommend to the legislature, from time to time, such additions and amendments to the laws as are deemed necessary for perfecting the school system of the state;

III. To appoint the state superintendent of public instruction;

IV. To appoint the county superintendents of the several counties of the state, subject to the approval of the board of chosen freeholders of the several counties at their first meeting after the appointments by the state board; but in

---

* By act of March 2d, 1875.

[See sec. 19a.] all cases where no action is taken by any board of chosen freeholders, approving or disapproving, then the appointments made by the state board shall be valid without such approval;

V. To prescribe all rules and regulations for holding teachers' institutes;

VI. To order all necessary repairs to the grounds, buildings and furniture of the state normal school, and to keep said buildings and furniture insured, and the comptroller shall draw warrants for the payment of the same, upon the certificate of the president of said board;

VII. To authorize the payment by the state treasurer, upon the warrant of the state comptroller, of all the necessary incidental expenses incurred by the state superintendent in the performance of his official duties;

VIII. To decide all appeals from the decision of the state superintendent of public instruction.

Compensation. 3. The members of the board shall receive no compensation for their services, but the state treasurer shall pay the necessary expenses of the said members, upon the warrant of the state comptroller.

Annual report. 4. The board shall report annually to the legislature in regard to all matters committed to their care.

B.—STATE SUPERINTENDENT OF PUBLIC INSTRUCTION.

State Superintendent, how elected, term of office, salary. 5. The state superintendent of public instruction shall be elected by the state board of education, by ballot, and shall hold office during the pleasure of the board, not to exceed the term of three years, receiving annually a salary of three* thousand dollars; Proviso. *provided*, that nothing herein contained shall prevent his re-election.

Location of office. 6. He shall be required to have his office in the state house, at Trenton.

To carry out instructions of State Board. 7. It shall be his duty to carry out the instructions of the board, and to enforce all rules and regulations prescribed by them.

* By act of March 16th, 1876.

8. He shall be, ex officio, secretary of the board of education, president of the state association of school superintendents, and a member of the state board of examiners, and of all county and city boards of examiners. Officer ex officio.

9. He shall have the supervision of all the schools of the state receiving any part of the state appropriation, and shall be the general adviser and assistant of the county superintendents; he shall, from time to time, as he shall deem for the interests of the schools, address circular letters to said superintendents, giving advice as to the best manner of conducting schools, constructing school houses, furnishing the same, and procuring competent teachers. Supervision of schools.

10. The state superintendent, under the direction of the trustees of the school fund, shall apportion to the several counties the state school moneys to which each may be entitled, which apportionment shall be made in the ratio of the number of children between the ages of five and eighteen in the said counties, as ascertained by the last annual report of the state superintendent; he shall furnish to the state comptroller, and to the county superintendent and the county collector of each county, an abstract of such apportionment, and shall draw his order on the state comptroller for the amount to which each county is entitled, in favor of the county collector of said county. Apportionment of school moneys. [See sec. 80.]

11. He shall have power, and it shall be his duty, to direct and cause the county superintendent of any county, or any board of trustees or other school officers, to withhold from any officer or district, or teacher, that part of the state appropriation derived from the revenue of the state, until such officer, district or teacher shall have complied with the provisions of this act and its supplements relating to his, its or their duties, and with all the rules and regulations made in pursuance thereof by the state board of education; he shall forbid the payment of said part of the state appropriation to any district in which the school or schools have not been kept according to law, or in which a public school has not been kept for at least [nine] months during the year next preceding the demand for payment. Power of withholding school moneys. [See sections 18a, 26 and 92.] [See sec. 77.]

Blanks and forms, how furnished.

12. He shall prepare, and cause to be printed, suitable forms for making all reports and conducting all necessary proceedings under the school laws of this state, and shall transmit them to the local school officers and teachers; he shall cause all school laws to be printed in pamphlet form, and shall annex thereto forms for making reports and conducting school business.

To decide disputes.

13. He shall decide, subject to appeal to the state board of education, and without cost to the parties, all controversies or disputes that may arise under the school laws of the state or under the rules and regulations prescribed by the state board of education; the facts of which controversies or disputes shall be made known to him by written statements by the parties thereto, verified by oath or affirmation, if required, and accompanied by certified copies of all documents necessary to a full understanding of the question in dispute; and his decision shall be binding until a different decision shall be given by the state board of education.

To collect books and apparatus.

14. He shall preserve in his office such school books, apparatus, maps, charts, works on education, plans for school buildings, and other articles of interest to school officers or teachers, as may be secured without expense to the state.

To preserve school documents.

15. He shall file all school reports of this state and of other states which may be sent to his office, and shall keep a record of all the acts connected with his official duties, and preserve copies of all the decisions given by him.

Office seal.

16. He shall provide a seal, with suitable device, for use in his office, by which all his official acts and decisions may be authenticated.

Annual report.

17. He shall report to the state board of education, at its annual meeting in December of each year, a statement of the condition of the public schools and of all the educational institutions receiving support from the state, which report shall contain full statistical tables of all items connected with the cause of education that may be of interest to the school officers or people of the state, together with such plans and suggestions for the improvement of the

schools and the advancement of public instruction in the state as he shall deem expedient.

18. He shall, at the expiration of his term of office, deliver to his successor his official seal, together with all property, books and documents, maps, records, reports and other papers belonging to his office, or which may have been received by him for the use of his office.

Deliver property to successor.

18*a*. He shall (unless the state board of education shall, for good cause shown, otherwise direct), have power, and it shall be his duty, to direct and cause the county collector of any county to withhold from any county superintendent any portion of his salary until he has fully complied with the provisions of the act to which this is a supplement, or any of its supplements, relating to his duties; and (unless the state board of education shall, for good cause shown, otherwise direct,) it shall be his duty to direct and cause the county superintendent of any county, or any board of trustees or school officers, to withhold from any officer or district, or teacher, that part of the state appropriation derived from the revenue of the state, until such officer, district or teacher shall have complied with the provisions of the act to which this is a supplement, or any of its supplements, relating to his, its or their duties, and with all the rules and regulations made in pursuance of any of these acts by the state board of education; and by and with the advice and consent of the state board of education, he shall have power, and it shall be his duty, to suspend or revoke the license of any teacher when the county superintendent shall make formal report that such teacher does not possess the attainments or qualifications which are essential to his office, or that the school or department of a school, under the charge of such teacher, is suffering from his or her incompetency, or from his or her failure or inability to govern or instruct the children who are under his or her care.

Power of withholding school moneys. [See sections 11, 26 and 92.]

C.—COUNTY SUPERINTENDENTS.

19. The state board of education shall appoint for each county one person, as provided in the fourth provision of

County Superintendent, how appointed.

section two, of suitable attainments, as the county superintendent of the public schools for that county, who shall hold office during the pleasure of the board, not to exceed the term of three years; *provided*, that nothing herein contained shall prevent his re-appointment.

Proviso.

Appointment to be approved by board of freeholders.

19*a*. The state board of education shall appoint the county superintendents of the several counties in the state, subject to the approval of the board of chosen freeholders of the several counties; but in all cases where a month elapses and no action is taken by any board of chosen freeholders approving or disapproving, then the appointments made by the state board shall be valid without such approval.

Salary of County Superintendent. [See sec. 20*a*.]

20. The yearly salary of the county superintendent shall be at the rate of ten cents for each child in the county between the ages of five and eighteen, as ascertained from the last annual report of the state superintendent, which salary shall be paid by the county collector, on the warrant of the state superintendent; *provided*, that the salary shall in no case be less than five hundred dollars, nor more than twelve hundred dollars; *and, provided*, that in case any city shall have a city superintendent of schools, who is not also the county superintendent, the children belonging to such city shall not be counted in determining the salary of the county superintendent, and the supervision of the schools of said city, which would otherwise belong to the county superintendent, shall devolve upon the city superintendent.

Proviso.

Proviso.

Expenses of County Superintendents.

20*a*. In order to enable county superintendents of schools to discharge their duties with greater efficiency, they shall receive annually, in addition to the salary now allowed them, such sums as they may need to pay the actual expenses incurred by them in the performance of their official duties, which sums shall be paid by the collector of the county, on the order of the state superintendent of public instruction; *provided*, that no such order shall be given in favor of any county superintendent until such county superintendent shall have furnished the state board of education a certified statement, under oath, by items, of the

Proviso.

expenses he has incurred, and that, during the year for which such order is drawn, he has performed faithfully all the duties imposed by the school law and by the regulations of the state board of education; *and provided further*, that in no case shall the expenses aforesaid exceed three hundred dollars annually; and after the passage of this act the salaries received by the county superintendents shall be determined by the school census report for the year eighteen hundred and seventy. **Proviso.** **Salary.**

Sections 21 and 22.*

23. He shall issue orders on the county collector in favor of each township collector and of each city treasurer, for that portion of the state appropriation to which said township or city is entitled; and shall file with each township collector and the clerk of each school district in any township, a copy of the apportionment of the township school funds made by him for said township, within twenty days after making said apportionment. **County Superintendent to issue orders. [See sec. 81.]**

24. He shall examine and license teachers, fix the boundaries of school districts, divide and unite districts, form new districts, provide for graded schools, and discharge other duties of general supervision and superintendence over the public schools of the county, in accordance with the regulations prescribed from time to time by the state board of education; but no school district shall hereafter be formed which shall contain less than seventy-five children between five and eighteen years of age; and each incorporated city or town shall hereafter constitute but one school district for all school purposes, and such consolidated district shall hold all the property and be liable for all the lawful debts of the district so consolidated. **License teachers, and change district bounds.**

25. He shall have power, and it shall be his duty, to appoint trustees for any district which, for any cause, fails to elect at the regular time; to appoint trustees to fill vacancies; to appoint the first trustees for any new district; *provided, however*, that when a new district is organized, such of the trustees of the old district as reside within the limits of the new one shall be trustees of the **Appointment of trustees.** **Proviso.**

*The provisions of sections 21 and 22 are contained in section 81.

new one, and the vacancy in the old district shall be filled by his appointment.*

Power of withholding school moneys. [See sections 11, 18*a* and 92.]

26. He shall have power to withhold that part of the state appropriation derived from the revenue of the state, from any district in which the inhabitants fail to provide a suitable school building and outhouses, or in which the existing buildings shall be pronounced by him and a majority of the trustees unfit for use; and for that purpose he may serve a notice on the township collector to withhold the payment of the same from such district.

Appointment of student for Agricultural College.

27. It shall be the duty of the county superintendent, at such time and place as the state superintendent may appoint, to examine such candidates for state scholarships at the agricultural college, as may present themselves, and the candidates shall be subjected to such examination as the faculty of the said college and the state superintendent shall prescribe; and the candidates who shall receive certificates of appointment to the agricultural college in any one county, shall be those who obtain, on such examination, the highest average for scholarship; and the number of certificates thus granted shall in no case exceed the number of state scholarships to which such county is entitled.

To give advice.

28. In all controversies arising under the school law the opinion and advice of the county superintendent shall first be sought, and from him appeal may be made, if necessary, to the state superintendent of public instruction.

State Association of School Superintendents.

29. The county and city superintendents shall together constitute an association, to be called "The State Association of School Superintendents," which association shall meet annually, at such times and places as the state board of education may appoint, and at such other times as they may agree upon.

Annual report by County and City Superintendents.

30. Each county superintendent, and each city superintendent, on or before the first of October of each year, shall make an annual report to the state superintendent, in the manner and form prescribed by him; which report

*The office of trustee is not vacated by an unaccepted resignation. *Townsend* v. *Trustees, &c.*, 12 Vr. 312.

shall specifically set forth any and all such facts within his purview as touch and describe the location and capacity of each school healthfully to accommodate the pupils in attendance, to the end that a full observation may be deduced, favorable or otherwise, as to an ample supply of sittings, suitability of conveniences, eligibility of position, attention to ventilation, and as to all such other pertinent subjects as may clearly and fully exhibit the sanitary condition of the public schools under his official inspection.

D.—SCHOOL TRUSTEES.

31. An annual meeting for the election of school trustees shall be held in each district on the Tuesday of the week following the annual town meeting, at the district school house, if there be one, and, if there be none, at a place to be designated by the district clerk, who shall post notices thereof, specifying the day, time, object and place of such meeting, in at least three public places in the district, one of which shall be at the school house, if there be one, at least ten days previous to the time of meeting; the voters shall be legal voters of the district, and a plurality of votes shall elect; and no person shall be eligible to the office of trustee unless he is a resident in the district; and further, no person shall be eligible to the office of school trustee unless he or she can read and write; but women who are residents in the district, and over the age of twenty-one years, shall also be eligible to the office of school trustee, and may hold such office, and perform the duties of the same, when duly elected by the legal voters of the district; *provided*, that the term of office of any trustee which would otherwise expire on the first or second day of July in any year, shall expire on the Tuesday of the week following the annual town meeting of the same year.*

Trustees, when and how elected.

Proviso.

31*a*. The township boards of trustees of the several townships of this state shall meet semi-annually, at such times and places as the county superintendent may appoint.

Meetings of township boards.

32. In all districts in which elections have been previ-

*Act of February 21st, 1882. This act also repeals all special acts relating to districts in townships inconsistent with the provisions of sections 31 and 36.

ously held, one trustee shall be elected for the term of three years, and if there are vacancies to be filled a sufficient number shall be elected to fill them for the unexpired terms.

Trustees for new districts.

33. In new districts acting under trustees appointed by the county superintendent, three trustees shall be elected for one, two and three years, respectively.*

District Clerk, how elected.

34. Each board of trustees shall, within ten days after the annual election, meet at the school house, or at some other convenient place, and proceed to elect one of their number clerk of the board, who shall be known and referred to as "district clerk;" and on their failure to do so the county superintendent shall appoint said clerk.

Duties of District Clerk.

35. He shall record, in a suitable book, all proceedings of the board, and of the annual school meetings, and of special school meetings, and pay out, by orders on the township collectors, in the manner prescribed by law, all school moneys of the district received from the state, township or district; he shall keep a correct and detailed account of all expenditures of school moneys in his district, and report the same to the county superintendent, and also to the township committee; at each annual school meeting he shall present his record book and his accounts for public inspection, and shall make a statement of the financial condition of the district and of the action of the trustees.

School census.

36. He shall take annually, or the board shall cause to be taken, during the month of May, an exact census of all children residing in the district between the ages of five and eighteen, not including the children who may be inmates of poorhouses, asylums or almshouses, and shall specify the names and ages of such children, and the names of their parents or guardians (all children who may be absent from home, attending colleges, boarding schools and private seminaries of learning, shall be included in the census list of the city, town or district in which their parents or guardians reside, and not be taken by the district clerk of the city, town or district where they may be attending such institutions of learning); and that he, or the person authorized to take the same, shall

*Balance of section repealed by act of March 14th, 1879.

make a full report thereof, verified by him under oath or affirmation, that the same is correct and true to the best of his knowledge and belief, on the blanks furnished for that purpose, to the county superintendent, on or before the first day of September next after his appointment, and keep a copy of the same for the use of the school trustees, and shall receive for his services such compensation as the board of trustees may allow.* Oath or affirmation. [See sec. 99.]

36*a*. From and after the passage of this act, in all cities wherein there now are, or may hereafter be, school boards, boards of education, or boards of school trustees, the enumeration and census of the children of school age in such cities shall be made and taken annually, on or before the first day of June, by the clerk or secretary of said boards, or by such other person or persons as may be appointed by said boards for such purposes, and a report thereof, duly attested by affidavit as correct, filed with the board of education or school trustees, who shall procure the same to be reported to the county superintendents of their respective counties.† Census of school children in cities.

36*b*. The enumeration and census so as aforesaid made and taken, shall contain the name in full and age of each child, and the name and residences of their parents, and the person or persons making the said census and reporting the same shall be entitled to such price, not less than three nor more than five cents, as may be fixed by the said school boards.† Census, how taken. Fee for each name.

37. He shall keep the school buildings in repair; he shall provide the necessary fuel, and obtain for the schools such supplies of crayons for blackboards, for the use of the pupils, as are necessary in carrying out the course of study prescribed therein; which repairs and supplies shall be paid for out of the moneys raised by the district. Fuel and supplies.

38. Every school district shall be known by the name and number assigned to it by the county superintendent, in accordance with the general regulations of the state board of education, and the trustees thereof shall be a body corporate, to be called and known by the name of "The Name and number of districts.

*Act of February 21st, 1882.
†Act of March 10th, 1880.

Trustees of School District Number ——, in the County of ———," and shall be capable of suing and being sued in all courts and places whatever, and of purchasing, holding and conveying real and personal property for the use and benefit of the schools of such district, and may have a corporate seal.*

Power of trustees.

39. The board of trustees of any school district shall have power, and it shall be their duty:

I. To employ and dismiss teachers, janitors, mechanics and laborers, and to fix, alter, allow and order paid their salaries and compensations;†

II. To make and enforce rules and regulations, not in conflict with the general regulations of the state board of education, for the government of schools, pupils and teachers;

III. To erect, enlarge, repair or improve school buildings, and purchase, lease, mortgage or sell school lots or school houses; to borrow money with or without mortgage, and to raise money by taxation for any such purpose, or to pay debts incurred therefor, or for the current expenses of any schools; *provided*, that for any such acts they shall have the previous authority of a vote of the district;

Proviso.

IV. To rent, furnish and repair school buildings, and keep the same insured;

V. To purchase personal property, and to receive, lease and hold in fee, in trust for their district, any and all real or personal property, for the benefit of the schools thereof;

VI. To enforce the regulations prescribed by the state board of education, and, in connection with the county superintendent, to prescribe the course of study to be pursued, and a uniform series of text-books to be used in the school or schools under their charge;

VII. To suspend or expel pupils from school;

VIII. To provide books for indigent children;

* The action must be brought against the district by its corporate name, and not against the trustees in their individual names, with description appended of "Trustees, &c." *Sproul* v. *Smith*, 11 Vr. 314. The trustees of a school district, in their corporate capacity, are not liable to be sued in a justice's or district court. *Townsend* v. *Trustees, &c.*, 12 Vr. 312; *Trustees, &c.*, v. *Stocker*, 13 Vr. 115.

† The employment of teachers by school corporations is an act judicial in its character, and should be done at a meeting of the trustees, of which all should have notice and have opportunity to participate in. *Townsend* v. *Trustees, &c.*, 12 Vr. 312.

IX. To require all pupils to be furnished with suitable books, as a condition of membership in the school;

X. To require every teacher to keep a state school register;

XI. To call a special meeting of the legal voters of the district at any time when, in the judgment of said trustees, the interests of the school may require it, which meeting shall be called in the manner provided in section eighty-[six] of this act for calling the annual district meeting, and no business shall be transacted at such special meeting except such as has been set forth in the notices by which said meeting was called;*

XII. To permit a school house to be used for other than school purposes, when a majority of the trustees present shall so agree at a meeting regularly called for that purpose;

XIII. To make an annual report, on or before the first of September, to the county superintendent, in the manner and form prescribed by the state superintendent of public instruction.

Meetings of township boards of trustees. [See sec. 31a.]

40. The district trustees of each township shall together constitute an association, to be called "The Township Board of Trustees;" said board shall meet at such times and places as the county superintendent may appoint, for the purpose of hearing from him communications and suggestions in regard to the management of the schools, and of submitting to him questions for advice or opinion relating to the same.

E.—TEACHERS.

School register, how kept.

41. Every teacher of a public school shall keep a school register in the manner provided therefor, and no salary shall be paid to such teacher until said register is exhibited to the district clerk or other officer authorized to make payment, and until said officer finds, by examination, that

* A special meeting of the legal voters of a school district, duly called, may vote to raise money for school purposes, although such appropriation has been refused at the annual meeting. *State, Trustees, &c.*, v. *Lewis*, 6 Vr. 377. Special meetings of the voters of a school district cannot be called unless ordered by the board of trustees regularly convened. *Bogert* v. *Trustees, &c.*, 14 Vr. —.

the register has been properly kept for the time for which salary is demanded, and enters upon the register a certificate to that effect.*

School register left with District Clerk.

42. Every teacher who shall leave a school before the close of the school year shall, at the time of leaving, make to the county superintendent a report of the school for all that portion of the current school year that the school has been in his or her charge, and shall, at the same time, give a duplicate of said report, and surrender the school register to the district clerk; and any teacher who may be teaching any school at the close of the school year shall, in his or her annual report, include all the statistics from the school register for the entire school year, notwithstanding any previous report for a part of the year; no school money shall be paid to any teacher for the last month of his or her services, until the report herein required shall have been made and received, and the register exhibited; *provided*, that in graded schools, in which there are more teachers than one, the principal teacher alone shall be responsible for the school report and register.

Proviso.

Teachers' certificate.

43. No teacher shall be entitled to any salary unless such teacher shall be the holder of a proper teacher's certificate in full force and effect.

School month and holidays.

44. In every contract, whether written or verbal, between any teacher and board of trustees, a school month shall be construed and taken to be twenty school days, or four weeks of five school days each; and no teacher shall be required to teach school on Christmas day, the first day of January, the fourth day of July, and such days of fasting or thanksgiving as may be appointed by the president of the United States or the governor of this state; and no deduction from the teacher's time or wages shall be made by reason of the fact that a school day happens to be one of the days referred to in this section; any contract made in violation of this section shall have no force or effect as against the teacher.

* A school teacher who has rendered services according to the requirements of the school law, and is refused compensation out of the fund specially provided for that purpose, is entitled to a mandamus to compel the proper officers to perform their duty, and to make payment of what is justly due. *Apgar* v. *School Trustees, &c.*, 5 Vr. 308.

45. Every teacher shall have power to hold every pupil accountable in school, for any disorderly conduct on the way to or from school, or on the play grounds of the school, or during recess, and to suspend from school any pupil for good cause; *provided*, that such suspension shall be reported by the teacher to the trustees as soon as practicable; and if such action is not sustained by them, the teacher may appeal to the county superintendent, whose decision shall be final.

Teacher's authority over pupils.

Proviso.

46. In case of the dismissal of any teacher before the expiration of any contract entered into between such teacher and trustees, the teacher shall have the right of appeal to the county superintendent, and if the county superintendent shall decide that the removal was made without good cause, said teacher shall be entitled to compensation for the full time for which the contract was made; but it shall be optional with the trustees whether he or she shall or shall not teach for the unexpired term.

Dismissal of teacher.

F.—PUPILS.

47. The pupils of the public schools shall comply with the regulations established in pursuance of law for the government of such schools; shall pursue the course of study and use the series of text-books prescribed by the trustees and county superintendent, and shall submit to the authority of the teacher; continued and willful disobedience, or open defiance of the authority of the teacher, the use of habitual profanity or obscene language, shall constitute good cause for suspension or expulsion from school; any pupil who shall in any way cut, deface or otherwise injure any school-house, fences or outbuildings thereof, shall be liable to suspension and punishment, and the parents of such pupil shall be liable for damages to the amount of injury, on complaint of the teacher, the amount to be determined by the trustees, and collected by the district clerk, by an action in debt therefor, in any court having jurisdiction, in his name as district clerk, together with the costs of said action.

Pupils to submit to authority of teacher.

G.—BOARDS OF EXAMINERS.

State Board of Examiners.

48. There shall be a state board of examiners, consisting of the state superintendent of public instruction and the principal of the state normal school; they shall have power, and it shall be their duty, to hold examinations of teachers, and to grant state certificates, or revoke the same, under such rules and regulations as the state board of education may prescribe; and a certificate thus granted shall entitle the holder, without further examination, to teach in any part of the state, so long as the certificate remains valid by the terms thereof, and in any school not of a higher grade than that for which the certificate represents him as qualified.

County Boards of Examiners.

49. There shall be in each county a county board of examiners, which shall be composed of the county superintendent, who shall, ex-officio, be chairman, and of a number of teachers, not to exceed three, to be appointed by him, who shall hold office for one year from the time of their respective appointments; but no person shall be appointed as county examiner unless he holds either a state or a first grade county certificate; the county superintendent shall fill vacancies that occur from absence or other causes, but if he cannot find any teacher in his county qualified, under the provisions of this section, willing to serve, he shall conduct the examination himself; the board shall meet at such times and places as may be designated by the chairman, and shall hold a session at least as often as once in every three months, and at the place and during the session of any teachers' institute held in the county; each member of the board, except the county superintendent, shall be paid for his services, in addition to his traveling expenses, a sum not exceeding three dollars for each session of said board, to be paid by the county collector on the order of the county superintendent; *provided*, that this compensation shall be paid only for the regular quarterly examinations; and that whenever said board shall hold sessions at any other time, no compensation shall be allowed from the county; but in cases of such special

Proviso.

examinations, said board may charge each applicant an examination fee not exceeding two dollars; the county board of examiners shall have power to conduct examinations and to grant certificates of different grades, in accordance with the general regulations on the subject prescribed by the state board of education, and the highest grade of certificate thus granted shall entitle the holder, without further examination, to teach in any part of the state so long as this certificate remains valid, and in any school not of a higher grade than that for which the certificate represents the holder as qualified; any county certificate lower than the highest grade will only entitle the holder to teach a school of a corresponding grade in the county, for which such certificate was granted.

50. In every city having a board of education governed by special laws, there shall be a city board of examiners, to consist of such members as said board of education of that city may appoint; said examiners shall have power, subject to such rules and regulations as may be prescribed by the city board of education, to grant certificates of qualification, which shall be valid for all schools of that city; and no teacher shall be employed in any of the schools of that city unless possessing such certificate, or a state certificate, nor in any school of a higher grade than that for which said certificate represents the holder to be qualified; any city board of examiners may recognize the certificates of any other city, and, without examination, issue to the holders certificates of a corresponding grade. City Boards of Examiners.

H.—SCHOOLS.

State Normal School.

51. There shall be a normal school, or seminary, for the training and education of teachers in the art of instructing and governing the common schools of this state, the object of which normal school or seminary shall be the training and education of its pupils in such branches of knowledge, and such methods of teaching and governing, as will qualify them for teachers of our common schools. Normal Schoo

Trustees, how appointed.

52. There shall be a board of trustees of said normal school, to consist of two trustees from each congressional district; the trustees already appointed shall continue in office severally for the terms for which they have been appointed, namely, seven whose terms expire in eighteen hundred and seventy-four, and seven whose terms expire in eighteen hundred and seventy-five; and annually thereafter, in the place of those whose terms are about to expire, the governor shall nominate, and by and with the advice and consent of the senate shall appoint, one trustee of said school from each congressional district, to hold office severally for the term of two years and until their successors are appointed, so that there shall always be two trustees from each congressional district; and in case of any vacancy by death, resignation or otherwise, a successor for the unexpired term shall in like manner be appointed; the state superintendent of public instruction shall be, ex officio, a member of said board of trustees.

52*a*. A quorum of the board of trustees of the state normal school shall consist of six members.*

Compensation.

53. The said trustees shall receive no compensation for their services, but the expenses necessarily incurred by them in the discharge of their duties shall be defrayed out of the funds hereinafter appropriated for the support of said school.

Supervision of Normal School.

54. To the said board of trustees shall be committed the control and use of the buildings and grounds owned and used by the state for the use of the normal school, the application of the funds for the support thereof, the appointment of teachers and the power of removing the same, the power to prescribe the studies and exercises of the school and rules for its management; to grant diplomas; to appoint some suitable person treasurer of the board, and to frame and modify, at pleasure, such by-laws as they may deem necessary for their own government; and they shall report annually to the legislature their own doings and the progress and condition of the school.

Number of pupils.

55. The number of pupils shall not exceed three for each

* By act of March 2d, 1875.

member of the senate and general assembly, and each county shall be entitled to fill three times as many seats in the school as it has representatives in the legislature; the applicants shall give, on admission, a written declaration, signed with their own hands, that their object in seeking admission to the school is to qualify themselves for the employment of public school teachers, and that it is their intention to engage in that employment in this state for at least two years.

55*a*. The applicants for admission to the normal school shall give, on admission, a written obligation, signed by their own hands, that their object in seeking admission to the school is to qualify themselves for the employment of public school teachers, and that it is their intention to engage in that employment in this state for at least two years, or refund to the state the cost of their tuition; and, in addition to the annual sum appropriated to the support of the normal school, there is hereby appropriated annually the sum of five thousand dollars, to be paid out of the treasury of the state in like manner, which shall constitute a scholarship fund, to be applied as follows: there shall be fifty scholarships of one hundred dollars each, two of which shall be allotted to each county, to be competed for by the pupils in the normal school from that county, and the remainder shall be open to free competition by pupils in the normal school from the state at large; the competitive examinations above mentioned shall be conducted by the principal of the state normal school and his assistants; *provided*, that scholarships shall be awarded to those pupils only who shall first enter into a satisfactory bond to the treasurer of the state, obligating themselves to teach in the public schools of this state for the term of five consecutive years, or to refund the amount paid them upon a failure to do so from any cause save continued sickness or death; *provided*, that until such system of scholarships shall be perfected by the board of trustees of the state normal school, said scholar's life fund shall be paid toward and for such purposes connected with the state normal school and boarding-house property belonging to the state as, in the

Scholarship fund.

Proviso.

Proviso.

judgment of said trustees, will be for the best interest of the state and the advantage of the cause of education.

Pupils, how admitted.

56. At the opening of each term of the normal school, the principal, with his assistants, shall proceed to examine applicants, and to admit to the school such as appear to be possessed of the proper qualification, to the number to which each county may be entitled.

Vacancies, how filled.

57. In case any county is not fully represented, additional candidates may be admitted from other counties, on sustaining the requisite examination.

Teachers, how appointed.

58. The board of trustees shall appoint and procure the number of teachers which may be necessary to carry out, in the best and highest sense, the purposes and designs of this act, and shall furnish for the use of the pupils the necessary apparatus and text-books, so far as the funds hereafter to be named and appropriated for the support of the school will allow; and the tuition in the normal school shall be gratuitous.

Model School.

59. The board of trustees are authorized to maintain a model school, under permanent teachers, in which the pupils of the normal school shall have opportunity to observe and practice the modes of instruction and discipline inculcated in the normal school, and in which pupils may be prepared for the normal school.

Appropriation.

60. For the support of the normal school, and to carry out the purpose and designs of this act, there is appropriated hereby the annual sum of fifteen thousand dollars, to be paid out of the treasury of the state upon the warrant of the comptroller.

School year for Normal School.

60*a*. The school year, so far as regards the state normal school, shall hereafter terminate on the last day of June.

Graded Schools.

Graded schools, how established.

61. Any two or more districts, by a majority vote of the inhabitants at a meeting regularly called or advertised by the county superintendent, or superintendents of the county or counties in which said districts are situated, may cause to be established and maintained a graded school,

which shall be entitled, according to the number of children in attendance, to its proper share of the state appropriation and of the township school taxes belonging to the districts which have caused said graded school to be erected; and a school thus established shall be governed by a joint board, combined of the trustees of the combining districts, and subject to such regulations as they may prescribe.

District Schools.

62. The inhabitants of every school district shall be required to provide a suitable school building and outhouses for the accommodation of their children; and in case such buildings are not provided, or those already in use shall be pronounced by the county superintendent and a majority of the trustees of said district unfit for the purposes for which they are applied, such district shall be deprived of the benefit of that part of the state appropriation derived from the revenues of the state until suitable buildings shall be erected. Suitable school buildings required.

63. No school district shall be entitled to receive any part of the school appropriation which shall not have maintained a public school for at least [nine] months during the then next preceding school year; *provided*, that any new district, or a district in which the school is discontinued on account of the repairing of an old or the erection of a new school building, shall not be deprived of its full share of the public school funds on account of the restrictions of this section. Time schools must be maintained. [See sec. 77.] Proviso.

64. The school year shall begin on the first day of September and end on the last day of August. School year.

I.—REVENUE AND APPORTIONMENT.

State Appropriations.

65. The governor of this state, the president of the senate, the speaker of the house of assembly, the attorney-general, the secretary of state and the comptroller, and Trustees of School Fund.

their successors in office, be and they are hereby constituted and appointed trustees of the fund for the support of public schools in this state, arising either from appropriations heretofore made, or which may hereafter be made by law, or which may arise from the gift, grant, bequest or devise of any person or persons whatsoever, which trustees shall be known by the name, style and title of "The Trustees for the Support of Public Schools;" *provided*, that it shall not be lawful for any teacher, trustee or trustees to introduce into or have performed in any school receiving its proportion of the public money, any religious service, ceremony or forms whatsoever, except reading the Bible and repeating the Lord's Prayer.

Proviso.

School Fund, how constituted.

66. The public stocks and moneys heretofore appropriated by law shall constitute the funds in the hands of the trustees appointed by the foregoing section of this act, and shall be held by the said trustees in trust, the interest and dividends arising therefrom to be applied by the said trustees, or a majority of them, for the support of public schools in this state, in the mode now prescribed or hereafter to be prescribed by any act or acts of the legislature, and for no other use or purpose whatsoever.

Money derived from sale of lands added to School Fund.

67. All moneys hereafter received from the sales and rentals of the land under water belonging to this state, shall be paid over to the trustees of the school funds and appropriated for the support of free public schools, and shall be held by them in trust for that purpose, and shall be invested by the treasurer of the state, under their direction, in the same manner as the funds now held by them are invested; the same to constitute a part of the permanent school fund of the state, and the interest thereof to be applied to the support of public schools, in the mode which now is, or hereafter may be, directed by law, and to no other use or purpose whatever.

Money derived from leases added to School Fund.

68. All leases which shall hereafter be made of lands belonging to the state, now or formerly lying under water, or which have been made since the sixth day of April, eighteen hundred and seventy-one, shall be transferred to the trustees of the school fund of this state, and become a

portion of the free school fund; and that the annual income arising from said leases shall be distributed by the said trustees for the support of free public schools, in the same manner that other moneys are now distributed for that purpose.

69. The fund above mentioned, together with all the moneys which shall be received by the treasurer in payment of the principal or interest of the bank or turnpike stock belonging to the fund for the support of free schools, all the taxes which may hereafter be received into the treasury from any of the banking and insurance companies in this state, the capital stock of which now is, or hereafter may be, liable by law to be taxed, all appropriations to said funds made or to be made by any law of this state, and the amount of all gifts, grants, bequests or devises hereafter made by any person or persons to the said trustees for the purposes contemplated by this act, shall be invested by the treasurer of this state, under the direction of the said trustees, or a majority of them, in the bonds of the United States or of New Jersey, or in bonds secured by mortgage on land in New Jersey, the interest thereof to be applied to the support of the public schools, in the mode which now is or may hereafter be directed by law, and to no other use or purpose whatsoever; an account of the management of the said fund shall be laid before the legislature with the annual statement of the treasurer's account; and no compensation shall be paid to said trustee or treasurer for any services performed in pursuance of the directions of this act; and all investments of money and property belonging to said fund now held or existing in the name of "The Trustees for the Support of Free Schools," are hereby and shall hereafter be vested in and held, and any proceedings or action whatever relative thereto may be taken, had, made and maintained by said trustees, in the name of the trustees for the support of public schools.

Investment of School Fund.

69*a*. The "Trustees for the Support of Public Schools" be and they are hereby authorized and empowered to bid for and purchase any lands and premises exposed to sale under the order and decree of any court, for the payment

Trustees for the support of public schools may purchase and hold lands and premises sold to satisfy claim, held by them.

and satisfaction of any mortgage encumbrance thereon held by the said trustees, and to take and hold the title to the land and premises so purchased in and by their official name, style and title, and as part of the assets of the school fund of New Jersey; *provided*, that said trustees shall not bid a higher price for such lands and premises than shall be sufficient to save the amount due upon their said mortgage encumbrance and costs, the taxed costs attending such proceedings and sale, if any, to be paid by the treasurer of this state out of the state funds, on warrant of the comptroller, and not out of the school fund.*

Proviso.

May sell and convey any lands and premises so purchased.

69*b*. The said "Trustees for the Support of Public Schools" be and they are hereby empowered and directed to sell and convey to any purchaser any lands and premises by them acquired under the provisions of this act, at such time, for such prices and on such terms of payment as the governor of this state for the time being shall, in writing under his hand, approve, and the consideration received therefor shall be assets of the school fund of this state.*

Trustees authorized to invest income of School Fund in public bonds.

69*c*. Whenever in the judgment of the trustees for the support of free schools of this state, or a majority of them, it shall not be deemed advisable or for the best interests of the school fund to invest the income of the said fund in bonds secured by mortgage on land, they shall have power to invest the said income or any portion thereof in the bonds of the United States and of this state and of the several counties, townships, boroughs and cities of the same.†

Loans for building school houses.

70. The treasurer of this state, under the direction of "The Trustees for the Support of Public Schools," is authorized to invest the fund for the support of public schools in this state, in addition to the securities mentioned in the preceding section of this act, in the bonds of the several school districts of this state, and in the bonds of any city or municipality of this state, legally issued for the purpose of building school houses, either by authority of special acts of the legislature or by the consent of the inhabitants of the district, as hereafter herein provided for.

*Act of April 9th, 1875.

†Act of March 21st, 1878.

70*a*. The trustees for the support of public schools in this state, and the commissioners of the sinking fund of New Jersey, be and are hereby authorized and empowered to reduce the rate of interest on any loan made by them or their predecessors in office, to the rate of six dollars per annum for the forbearance of every one hundred dollars, from and after the fourth day of July next.* Rate o interest.

71. The treasurer of this state shall annually make and furnish to the board of trustees for the support of public schools, on the first day of the stated annual meeting of the legislature, and at such other times as the majority of the said trustees shall require the same, a particular statement of the school fund, containing an account of the securities belonging to said fund, with the dates of investment, their value, and the interest arising from each denomination of securities, together with an account of the moneys in the treasury belonging to said fund. Report concerning School Fund.

72. The secretary of state is hereby constituted and appointed secretary of the said board of trustees, whose duty it shall be to record, in a book to be kept for that purpose, the proceedings of the said board, and the accounts to be furnished by the treasurer as hereinbefore stated. Secretary.

73. It shall be the duty of the trustees of the school fund of this state, on or before the first Monday of April of every year, to appropriate out of the annual income of the fund for the support of public schools the sum of one hundred thousand dollars; and if the annual income of said fund shall not have been received in full, or shall be insufficient for that purpose, then the said trustees are hereby authorized and empowered to draw for any sum necessary to make up the deficiency, by warrant, signed by the comptroller, upon the treasurer of the state, who is directed to pay the same; which sum, so drawn from the treasury aforesaid, shall be replaced from the annual income of said school fund so soon as the same shall be received.† Appropriation of School Fund to schools.

Section 74 repealed.‡

* Joint Resolution of March 27, 1878.
† Act of March 27th, 1878.
‡ Act of March 27th, 1878.

Section 75.*

Teachers' Institutes.

76. For the purpose of defraying the expenses of teachers' institutes, the procuring of teachers and lecturers for said institutes, and other necessary expenses of the same, there may be paid, annually, to the state superintendent of public instruction, a sum not exceeding one hundred dollars to one teachers' institute in any county, or in any two or more adjoining counties of this state, the same to be paid out of the state treasury on the warrant of the comptroller, upon itemized accounts rendered to him by the state superintendent of public instruction of the expenses incurred.†

Taxation.

State tax imposed.

77. For the purpose of maintaining free public schools there shall be assessed, levied and collected annually upon the taxable real and personal property in this state, as exhibited by the latest abstracts of ratables from the several counties, made out by the several boards of assessors, and filed in the office of the comptroller of the treasury, a state school tax equal to four dollars for each child in this state between the ages of five and eighteen years, as exhibited by the next preceding school census; which tax shall be assessed, levied and collected at the same time and in the same manner in which other taxes are assessed, levied and collected; but if the moneys received by any township from the tax imposed by this act shall not be sufficient to maintain free schools for at least nine months in each year, then the inhabitants thereof may raise by township tax such additional amount as they may need for that purpose in the same manner as such taxes have heretofore been raised.‡

School nine months.

Township school tax.

Comptroller shall apportion tax among counties.

78. It shall be the duty of the comptroller aforesaid to apportion the said tax among the several counties, in proportion to the amount of taxable real and personal estate of said counties respectively, as shown by the ratables respectively as aforesaid, and it shall be his further duty to transmit, on or before the first day of April of each year,

Transmit statement.

* The provisions of section 75 are contained in section 10.

† Act of March 25th, 1881.

‡ Act of March 16th, 1881.

to the county collector of each county, a statement of the amount of said tax apportioned to and payable by said county, and said county collector shall lay said statement before the board of assessors of the townships and wards within his county at their next annual meeting, to apportion the taxes among said townships and wards, and said assessors shall thereupon proceed to apportion said school taxes as other taxes are apportioned, and to assess the same according to law.* Duties of assessors.

79. It shall be the duty of the county collectors of the several counties of this state to pay to the treasurer of this state the quotas due from their respective counties of the taxes imposed by this act, on or before the first day of January, annually, next ensuing the assessment thereof. State tax, when paid.

80. Ten per centum of the full amount of money annually raised by virtue of the seventy-seventh section of this act shall be known as a reserve fund, and shall be apportioned among the several counties of the state, by the state board of education, equitably and justly, according to their own discretion, on or before the fifteenth day of April subsequently to the aforesaid apportionment by the comptroller of the treasury; and it shall be the duty of the state superintendent of public instruction, on or before the tenth day of January next ensuing said apportionment, to draw orders on the comptroller of the treasury, and in favor of the county collectors, for the payment of ninety per centum of the amount of school tax paid by the counties respectively; and the said county collectors shall apply for and be entitled to receive the amount of said orders as soon as the same are received; and the said superintendent shall also draw his orders in favor of the respective county collectors, for such portion of the reserve fund as shall have been apportioned to the counties respectively, as aforesaid, which orders shall be payable when the said reserve fund has been paid by the several counties; *provided*, that no portion of said moneys shall be used for the support of sectarian schools.* State Board of Education shall apportion reserve fund among the counties. Proviso.

* Act of March 16th, 1881.

County Superintendents shall apportion moneys among the townships, cities and districts.

81. It shall be the duty of the county superintendent of each county to apportion annually to the districts and cities of his county the state school moneys, together with the interest of the surplus revenue belonging to said county, and such other moneys as may be raised for school purposes upon the basis of the last-published school census; *provided*, that all children residing in fractional districts, situated in two or more adjoining townships, shall be included in the census of that township in which the fraction containing the school house is situated; *and provided also*, that no district shall receive from all state and county funds less than two hundred dollars; and that districts with forty-five children or more shall not receive less than three hundred and fifty dollars.*

Proviso.

Proviso.

State Superintendent to give orders in favor of County Collectors.

82. The state comptroller, annually, after having received from the state superintendent of public instruction a statement of the apportionment of the state appropriation among the several counties, shall draw his warrant on the state treasurer in favor of the county collector of any county for the portions to which said county is entitled, whenever such county collector shall present an order for the same drawn by the state superintendent of public instruction in favor of such county.

County Superintendents to give orders in favor of Township Collectors.

83. The county collector of each county shall receive and hold in trust that part of the state appropriation belonging to his county, and shall pay out the same to the collectors of the several townships and to the city treasurer of the cities of his county, only on the orders of the county superintendent; *provided*, that in townships where there are less than two hundred children between the ages of five and eighteen, the inhabitants may raise such a sum per child as will be sufficient to maintain their schools.†

Proviso.

* Act of March 16th, 1881.

†(1) A county collector is not required or permitted to exercise any discretion as to how much of the state appropriation the several township collectors in the county are entitled to receive from him. That question as between these officers is settled conclusively by the order of the county superintendent of public schools. (2) The notion that a county collector can, in any case, lawfully reduce the amount by setting up some counter claim, whether in his own behalf or in behalf of his county, and whether against the township collector, personally, or against his township, is neither justified by the language nor consistent with the policy of our school laws. *State, Herder, &c.*, v. *Collector, &c.*, 7 Vr. 363.

84. It shall be the duty of the township collector of each township to receive and hold in trust all school moneys belonging to the township or to any of the districts thereof, whether received from the state appropriation, from township or district tax, or from other sources, and to pay out the same only on the orders of the district clerks of the several districts of his township, which order shall specify the object for which it is given, and shall be signed by at least one other trustee beside said clerk, and shall be made payable to the order of and be indorsed by the person entitled to receive it, and he shall, on the order of the township committee, pay over any balance of school funds remaining in his hands to his successor in office, and he shall procure a suitable book, in which he shall keep a separate account with each school district in his township, crediting each with the amounts apportioned to it by the county superintendent, and the amount raised by tax in the district, and charging each with the orders paid for said district, and he shall present his accounts to be examined and settled by the township committee at the close of the year, a copy of which settlement, certified by the committee, showing the amounts received, the amounts expended by him for school purposes during the year and the balance remaining in his hands; he shall transmit said copy within ten days to the county superintendent, and another copy of the same he shall file with the clerk of the township, and as compensation for such service the township collector shall be entitled to receive three-fourths of one per centum on all school funds received and paid out by him for such purposes during the year, to be paid by the township committee from the funds of the township.

Township Collectors to hold school moneys in trust.

To keep accounts of school moneys.

Report to Township Committee and to County Superintendent.

Compensation.

(1) The county collector of each county shall receive and hold in trust the state appropriation for public schools belonging to his county, and pay the same to the collectors of the several townships and to the city treasurers of the cities of his county only on the orders of the county superintendent, and is responsible for these moneys if otherwise expended. (2) School taxes are to be levied and applied for the fiscal year beginning September 1st, succeeding the assessment, and not for the preceding year. (3) A *mandamus* will be allowed for the payment of the county superintendent's order for the state appropriation for public schools, where the moneys have been applied for school purposes in the preceding year, beginning January 1st. *State ex rel. Board of Education, &c.*, v. *Sheridan, &c.*, 13 Vr. 64.

Fractional districts.

85. All school moneys belonging to fractional districts shall be held, subject to the order of the trustees, by the collector of that township in which the fraction containing the school house is situated.

Cities and districts may raise school tax.

86. In addition to the tax imposed by the seventy-seventh section of this act, each city and school district may raise by tax such other sums of money as they may need for school purposes, in the following manner, unless otherwise authorized by any special act applicable to such city school district:

Annual district meeting for ordering school tax.

The legal voters of such district are hereby authorized and required to meet on the Tuesday of the week following the annual town meeting, for the purpose of determining what additional school tax, if any, shall be levied upon the district; said meeting shall be held at some convenient public place within the district, and notice thereof, setting forth the time, place, and object of such meeting and the amount of money desired to be raised, shall be given by the district clerk, and set up in at least three public places within the district, ten days before the day of meeting; and the said inhabitants so met, shall have power, by the consent of a majority of those present, to authorize the trustees of said district to purchase land for school purposes, to build, enlarge, or repair a school-house or school-houses, and to borrow money therefor, or to sell or mortgage a school-house or school-houses, and to raise by taxation for these purposes, or to pay a debt of the district incurred for such purposes, and for the current expenses of the school or schools, such sum of money as a majority of the inhabitants so assembled shall agree to; and if at such meeting the trustees shall be authorized to borrow money not exceeding four hundred dollars in amount, to build or repair a school-house to cost less than five hundred dollars, such meeting may direct that the money to pay the debt so authorized to be raised by poll-tax, assessed upon the taxable inhabitants of said district, and that one hundred dollars, with interest, on the amount of said borrowed money remaining unpaid be so raised in each year, for a period of four years; and in case any money shall be ordered, by a vote of a majority of said meeting, to be raised by taxation, the district clerk shall make out and sign a certificate thereof, under oath or affirmation, that the same is correct and true, and deliver the same to the assessor or assessors of the township or townships in which said district is situate, and to the county superintendent, which said assessor or assessors shall assess on the inhabitants of said school district and their estates, and the taxable property therein, in the same manner as township taxes are assessed, such sum of money as shall have been ordered to be raised by the said meeting, in the manner aforesaid; and said money shall be assessed, levied, and collected; and it shall be the duty of the collector or collectors of the township or townships in which said district is situate, to pay over all moneys by him or them received, which shall have been assessed by virtue of such a vote of a district meeting as aforesaid, on the order of the district clerk of said district, to be used for the purposes directed by the district meeting so held as aforesaid; *provided*, that whenever any district school meeting shall be held as aforesaid, or at the call of the trustees, as provided in the eleventh division of the thirty-ninth section of this act, it shall not be lawful for such meeting to order a greater sum of money to be raised by district tax than shall have been mentioned and designated in the notice of such meeting set up in the manner required by law; *and provided further*, that whenever in the judgment of the trustees of any district it shall not be necessary to levy a district tax for school purposes, the district clerk thereof shall not set up the notices directed to be given as aforesaid.* † Proviso. Proviso.

86*a*. The several assessors and collectors of the townships and wards of this state shall be entitled to receive five cents, and no more, for each name for assessing, levying and collecting district school taxes.‡ Compensation to assessors and collectors.

* Act of March 14th, 1879.

† The resolution acted upon must specify which object or objects mentioned in this section for which the money voted is to be used. In case more than one of these purposes are mentioned the resolution must specify how much money is to be apportioned to each. *Cochrane* v. *Garrabrant, &c.*, 3 Vr. 441; *Banghart* v. *Sullivan*, 7 Vr. 89; *Corrigan* v. *Duryea*, 11 Vr. 266.

‡ Act of April 8th, 1875.

Districts may issue bonds.

87. It shall and may be lawful for the inhabitants of each district, when met in conformity to the provisions of the eighty-sixth section of this act, or at the call of the trustees, as provided in the eleventh division of the thirty-ninth section of this act; and the inhabitants so met shall have power, by the consent of a majority of those present, to authorize the trustees, for the purpose of purchasing land for school purposes, or for the purpose of building a school-house or school-houses in such district, to issue bonds of the district in the corporate name of such district, in such sums and in such amounts, and payable at such times as the inhabitants so met may direct, with interest at the rate of [six*] per cent. per annum, payable half-yearly, which bonds shall be signed by the trustees of such district and attested by the clerk, under the seal of the district, and the bonds so issued shall be a lien upon the property of the said district.†

Bonds a lien upon districts.

88. The bonds of the several school districts of this state, heretofere or hereafter legally issued for the purpose of building school-houses, shall be a lien upon the real and personal estates of the inhabitants of the said districts, as well as the property of the said districts; and the property of the inhabitants as well as the property of the districts, shall be liable for the payment of the same; *provided,* such bonds are [six*] per centum bonds, and the interest is payable semi-annually, and coupons shall be attached thereto; and that in all cases copies of all papers and proceedings authorizing the issuing of such bonds shall be submitted to the attorney-general for his approval of the legality of the same, who shall receive such compensation for the examination of the same as shall be fixed by the trustees for the support of public schools, which sum shall be paid by the districts seeking such loan.

Proviso.

Assessments for payments on bonds.

89. Whenever any district shall order and authorize the issue of bonds, for the purpose aforesaid, it shall be the duty of the district clerk of such district, each and every year, to issue the warrant of the district, signed by the

* By act of February 26th, 1878.
† Act of March 9th, 1877.

trustees, and attested by the clerk under the seal of the district, to the assessor or assessors of the township or townships in which such district is situate, directing him to assess upon the inhabitants of said school district, and their estates and the taxable property therein, an amount sufficient to pay the bond or bonds of the district, maturing in such year, together with the interest accruing upon the whole issue of the unpaid bonds of such district, which warrant so issued as aforesaid, shall be executed in the same way and manner as is provided by the eighty-sixth section of this act.

90. The several townships in this state are authorized and required to appropriate the interest of the surplus revenue received by them, and from other funds not raised by tax, such sums for the support of the public schools as they shall order and direct at their annual town meetings, in addition to the amount received from the state appropriation and the amount which they raise by tax. **Interest on surplus revenue appropriated to schools.**

J.—MISCELLANEOUS.

91. Not more than twenty dollars annually, of the school moneys received by any school district, except such as may be raised within the district, shall be used for any other purpose than the payment of teachers' salaries and for purchasing fuel. **Twenty dollars for incidentals.**

92. In case any school district or city shall use any of the school money apportioned to it for any other than public school purposes, as these purposes are defined and limited in the ninety-first section of this act, such district or city shall forfeit out of the next annual apportionment a sum equal to twice the amount thus used; and it shall be the duty of the county superintendent to reapportion the money thus forfeited among the other districts and cities of his county; *provided*, the state superintendent may remit such penalty for cause.* **Power of withholding school money. (See sections 11, 18a and 26.)** **Proviso.**

93. In case of the failure of any district clerk or city superintendent to send his annual report to the county **Penalty for failure by District Clerk to report.**

*Act of March 25th, 1881.

superintendent of his county in the form prescribed, on or before the first of September, such county superintendent shall make up his report for such district or city from the last published report of the state superintendent; in making up such report, however, he shall deduct one-fifth from the school census; *provided, however*, that all such cases of delay or negligence shall be reported to the state superintendent of public instruction, whose duty it shall be to investigate the same, and to restore the number deducted from the school census in all cases, when he receives satisfactory reasons for such delay or negligence.

Proviso.

Tuition fees not allowed.

94. It shall not be lawful to charge tuition fees for the support of public schools in this state, but that all such schools shall be free to all persons over five and under eighteen years of age residing within the district, so long as such schools can be thus maintained with the public school funds.

Library appropriation.

95. The treasurer of the state, upon the order of the state superintendent of education, is hereby authorized and directed to pay over the sum of twenty dollars out of any money that may be in the public treasury to every public school for which there shall have been raised by subscription or entertainment a like sum for the same purpose, to establish in such school a school library, and to procure philosophical and chemical apparatus; and the further sum of ten dollars annually, upon a like order, to the said public school, upon condition that there shall have been raised by subscription or entertainment a like sum for such year, for the purposes aforesaid.*

Selection of books.

96. The selection of books and apparatus shall be approved by the school trustees of such district.

Rules.

97. The school trustees of each district shall make proper rules and regulations for the management, use, and safe keeping of such libraries.

Corporal punishment forbidden.

98. No teacher shall be permitted to inflict corporal punishment upon any child in any school in this state.

County Superintendent authorized to administer oath.

99. The county superintendent shall have power to administer all necessary oaths or affirmations to district

* Act of April 5th, 1878.

clerks and other school officers, for which he shall receive no compensation.

100. All acts and parts of acts of a general character on the subject of public schools and of the normal school and its appropriations passed before the twenty-first day of March, one thousand eight hundred and sixty-seven, are hereby declared to be repealed. Repealer.

Approved March 27th, 1874.

SUPPLEMENT approved April ninth, eighteen hundred and seventy-five.

1. Every parent, guardian or other person having control and charge of any child between the ages of eight and fourteen years, shall cause such child to attend some public or private school, at least twelve weeks in each year, six weeks at least of which attendance shall be consecutive; or to be instructed at home at least twelve weeks in each year, in the branches of education commonly taught in the public schools, unless the physical or mental condition of the child is such as to render such attendance inexpedient or impracticable. Children shall attend school twelve weeks in each year, or be instructed at home for same period.

2. Any person failing to comply with the provisions of this act shall, on written notice of such failure from the district clerk of the school district, or the person designated by the board of education of the city where such offence has occurred, forfeit for the first offence, and pay to the township collector or city treasurer, the sum of two dollars; and after such first offence, shall, for each succeeding offence in the same year, forfeit and pay to the township collector or city treasurer, the sum of three dollars for each and every week, not exceeding twelve weeks in any one year, during which they, after written notice as aforesaid, shall have failed to comply with the provisions of this act. Penalty for non-compliance.

3. It shall be the duty of the district clerk of each school district, and of some person in each city to be selected by Duties of the District Clerk of each school district.

the city board of education, to report to the township collector of the township or city treasurer of the city where the offence has occurred, the names of all parents, guardians or other persons who fail to comply with the provisions of this act; and the officer to whom such report is made, shall proceed to collect the penalties imposed by this act, in any court of competent jurisdiction, in the county in which such city, town, township or school district may be situated; the said penalties, when paid, to be added to the public school money of said school district in which the offence occurred; *provided*, this law shall not be operative in those school districts of the state where there are not sufficient accommodations to seat the children compelled to attend school under the provisions of this act.

Proviso.

Extract from An Act concerning Disorderly Persons. (Revision.) Approved April ninth, eighteen hundred and seventy-five.

Persons injuring school property, or disturbing schools adjudged disorderly.

7. Any person who shall enter the buildings or go upon the lands belonging to any public school district of this state or used and occupied for school purposes by any public school in this state, and shall break, injure or deface such building or any part thereof, or the fences or outhouses belonging to or connected with such building or lands, or shall disturb the exercises of such public school, or molest or give annoyance to the children attending such school, or any teacher therein, shall be deemed and adjudged to be a disorderly person, and may be apprehended in the manner hereafter prescribed in this act, and taken before any justice of the peace of the county where such person may be apprehended; and it shall be the duty of the said justice to commit such disorderly person, when convicted before him by the confession of the offender, or by the oath or affirmation of one or more witness or witnesses, to the county jail of such county, there to be kept at hard labor for any term not exceeding thirty days.

Penalty.

SUPPLEMENT approved March nineteenth, eighteen hundred and seventy-four.

Whenever the trustees of any school district in Cumberland county shall be directed or authorized to purchase land for school purposes, to build, enlarge, or repair, or improve school buildings, or borrow, or raise money therefor, or to pay debts of the district, incurred for such purposes, or for the current expenses of the school, the vote of the inhabitants so directing or authorizing the trustees shall be taken by ballot. Vote to be taken by ballot in certain cases

SUPPLEMENT of an act for the Punishment of Crimes, approved February seventh, eighteen hundred and seventy-six.

If any board of chosen freeholders or any township committee, or any board of aldermen or common councilmen, or any board of education, or any board of commissioners of any county, township, city, town or borough, in this state, or any committee or member of any such board or commission, shall disburse, order or vote for the disbursement of public moneys, in excess of the appropriation respectively to any such board or committee, or shall incur obligations in excess of the appropriation and limit of expenditure provided by law for the purposes respectively of any such board or committee, the members thereof, and each member thereof thus disbursing, ordering or voting for the disbursement and expenditure of public moneys, or thus incurring obligations in excess of the amount appropriated and limit of expenditure as now or hereafter appropriated and limited by law, shall be severally deemed guilty of malfeasance in office, and on being thereof convicted, shall be punished by fine not exceeding one thousand dollars, or imprisonment at hard labor for any term not exceeding three years, or both, at the discretion of the court.

AN ACT concerning appropriations made by and to the boards of education in cities of this state, approved March ninth, eighteen hundred and seventy-seven.

Appropriations may be modified.

1. It shall be lawful for any board of education of any incorporated city of this state, from time to time, to modify the several appropriations made by the board, to be expended under the direction of its several committees during any fiscal year; *provided, however*, that said modifications shall not authorize any expenditure in excess of the sum appropriated for the current expenses of the department of public instruction at the time when such appropriation shall have been originally made.

Proviso.

Money appropriated for current expenses not to be otherwise used.

2. The amount appropriated by the board of aldermen or other body charged with the duty of making appropriations for defraying the current expenses of the department of public instruction of any city of this state, for each successive year, shall thereby become appropriated to defray such current expenses and shall be used for no other purpose whatever.

SUPPLEMENT approved March tenth, eighteen hundred and eighty.

Trustees of public schools, when to meet.

1. The trustees of the public schools, elected in each school district in this state, shall meet for the transaction of business connected with the public schools in their respective districts, on the first Tuesday after the first Monday in March, June, September and December, or oftener if the business of the board require it.

Bills and demands to be passed on in open session.

2. All bills and demands for money expended for school purposes, and all contracts entered into, shall be presented and passed on in open session of the board of school trustees, and no bills or demands for money on that account shall be paid which have not been thus passed on and approved.

3. It shall be unlawful for any board of school trustees or board of education of this state, to pay or disburse, out of the school moneys under their control, any sum for school supplies, books, maps, charts, globes, fuel, erecting, enlarging, repairing or improving school buildings and grounds, and janitors' salaries, unless the person claiming or receiving the said moneys shall first present to the board of trustees or boards of education, a detailed bill of items or demand, specifying particularly how such bill or demand is made up, and the dates thereof, and the names of the persons to whom the amount composing such bill or demand is due; *provided*, that the district clerk, as he may be authorized by the board of trustees, is empowered to purchase for the school or schools under their control, such supplies as may be necessary, and shall present an itemized bill of the same, with affidavit attached, which shall be acted on and paid as other bills; and said itemized bill shall be considered as satisfying all the provisions of this act. **Unlawful for trustees to pay any bills or demands unless the same are itemized.** **Proviso.**

4. Any person or persons presenting any such bill or demand, shall make an affidavit that the goods or services, itemized in said bill or demand, have been delivered or rendered, that no bonus has been given or received by any person or persons with the knowledge of the deponent in connection with the claim, and that the same is correct and true; *provided*, that the clerk of any board of trustees or board of education is hereby authorized to take said affidavit without cost. **Affidavit to be made to all bills.** **Proviso.**

5. Any board of school trustees or board of education, who shall wilfully violate the provisions of this act, shall be deemed guilty of a misdemeanor, and, on conviction thereof, shall be punished by a fine not to exceed one hundred dollars, or as the court may direct. **Penalty for violating this act.**

Extract from An Act concerning the protection of the public health, and the record of vital facts and statistics relating thereto, approved March eleventh, one thousand eight hundred and eighty.

10. At the enrollment of the children each year by the clerk of district schools or by other proper officers in cities, inquiry shall be made as to how many of the children within the school age are unvaccinated, and the same shall be designated by a mark on said roll, and in the case of any found unvaccinated whose parents desire them to be protected from small pox, but who, in the judgment of the board of education or the trustees of the school district, are not able to pay therefor, the school clerk or other authorized person may give to said child or children a permit to appear at the office of any regularly licensed physician of said school district or of said township to be vaccinated, and any such physician, on the presentation of such permit, with his certificate appended thereto that the said vaccination has been by him successfully performed, shall be entitled to receive from the township committee or city treasurer fifty cents for every such certified case.

AN ACT for building school houses in townships, approved March eleventh, eighteen hundred and eighty.

Lawful for school district to vote money and provide land.

1. From and after the passage of this act, it shall be lawful for any school district of this state, at their annual meeting, to vote money to build a school house, as money is now voted for said school district under any existing law, and to provide land for that purpose, not exceeding acres, at such place in the said school district as the school trustees thereof may designate, and for that purpose the said school trustees may acquire the said land by purchase or condemnation; *provided*, a majority of the taxable residents of said school district shall be present at any meeting

Proviso.

as aforesaid, and shall vote on any proposition presented for the selection of a place and voting money as aforesaid.

2. It shall be lawful for such school trustees to enter upon any lands and make all such preliminary examinations, explorations, measurements and levelings as may be necessary and proper for their purposes, doing thereby as little damage as possible to the owner or owners thereof.

School trustees may enter upon lands, &c.

3. In case said school trustees cannot agree with the owner or owners or other persons interested in any lands which said school trustees may desire to take, use and occupy, or from which they may desire to take or divert, either in whole or in part, for the purposes of their building, or cannot agree with the owner or owners for the whole or any part of any lands as to the amount of compensation to be paid for such taking, use, diversion or occupation or interest, it shall be lawful for any justice of the supreme court of this state, upon application by said school trustees, and upon two weeks' previous notice, served in person, or by leaving at the dwelling house or usual place of abode of such owner or owners, or in case of absence from the state or legal disability, published in a newspaper published nearest to the lands in question, to appoint three disinterested commissioners, residents of the county in which said lands are situated, to assess and ascertain the value of the lands so proposed to be taken, used and occupied, which commissioners shall appoint a time and place at which they shall meet to execute the duties of their appointment, and shall cause two weeks' notice thereof to be given to the parties interested therein, either by personal service or by publication in a newspaper published in the county where such lands may be, at which time and place the said commissioners shall meet and view the premises, and hear the parties interested, and take evidence, if any be offered, and for that purpose shall have power to administer oaths or affirmations, and to adjourn from day to day; and in case of the refusal or failure of either or any of said commissioners to attend and perform their said duties, the said judge shall have power to appoint another

Proceedings in case trustees and owner or owners cannot agree as to compensation for lands.

Justices of Supreme Court to appoint commissioners to ascertain and assess value of land.

Refusal to serve, Judge to appoint another.

or other disinterested person or persons as commissioners to act in the place of such absent commissioner or commissioners; and the said trustees shall make and exhibit to the said commissioners at their meeting aforesaid, for the use of the parties interested, a statement and description in writing, or by drawings or maps, or both, of the lands by them sought to be taken or diverted as aforesaid, and of the use, occupation of, and excavations upon any lands by them sought to be made; and the said commissioners shall thereupon ascertain and assess the value and damages aforesaid, and shall execute under their hands and seals, or the hands and seals of a majority of them, an award to said trustees of the lands, by them sought in the statements and description aforesaid, stating therein the amount of damages and compensation therefor by them assessed in favor of such owner or owners, which award shall be by them acknowledged and filed in the county clerk's office, and by him recorded; *provided, always*, that if any real estate, the owner or owners of which shall not have given his, her or their consent in writing to the diversion or to the taking of said land, shall not have been ascertained and paid pursuant to the directions of this act, shall be injured or damaged by the diversion or diminution of any said land that the owner or owners thereof may have and maintain his, her or their action to recover damages for such injury, which he, she or they may sustain by reason of anything done under this act, as if this act had not been passed.

Trustees to exhibit to commissioners a description, &c., of lands to be taken.

Commissioners to ascertain and assess the value, &c.

Proviso.

4. Before taking possession of any such lands, or entering thereon for the purpose of making any excavation or occupation thereof, or taking any interest in land as aforesaid, the said trustees shall pay or tender to such owner or owners, or, in case of absence from the state or legal disability, shall deposit with the clerk of the circuit court of said county the value and damages so awarded; and the award of said commissioners and the payment or tender or deposit as aforesaid of the same, shall vest in said corporation the lands by them sought, described and set forth in said statement and description, in all respects the same as if the same had

Trustees to pay owner the value and damages awarded.

Upon payment, &c., title to vest in the corporation.

been conveyed to said trustees by said owner or owners under their hands and seals.

5. If either party feel aggrieved by said assessment and award, such party may appeal to the next or second term of the circuit court of said county, by petition and notice thereof served upon the opposite party two weeks prior to such term, or published a like space in a newspaper published nearest the lands in question, which petition and notice so served or published shall vest in said courts full power to hear and determine said appeal, and, if required, they shall award a venire for a jury to come before them, who shall hear and finally determine the issue under the direction of the court, as in other trials by jury; and it shall be the duty of the said jury to assess the damages to the said lands as above mentioned, and the value of such lands as shall be absolutely taken; and said court shall have power to order a struck jury, or a jury of view, or both, to try any such appeal, and also to order any jury which may be empaneled and sworn to try any such appeal, to view the premises in question during said trial; and the right of said trustees to appeal from and dispute the correctness of any award, shall not be waived or taken away by the paying or tendering the amount of the award and taking possession of the land, or exercising the rights covered by such award; and the right of any owner of any such lands or rights in like manner to appeal, shall not be waived or lost by the acceptance of the amount so awarded, when tendered; and upon the final determination of any such appeal, the said court shall render such judgment in favor of the one party and against the other, as the right and justice of the case shall require, and shall award to the party substantially succeeding and prevailing in said appeal, his, her or their costs of said appeal against the opposite party, and shall have power to enforce the judgment so rendered by execution, as other judgments are enforced, and also by summary proceedings and attachments for non-payment thereof.

Parties aggrieved may appeal to the Circuit Court.

Court may order a struck jury to try any appeal.

Right of appeal not to be waived by acceptance of amount awarded.

An Act relative to Boards of Education in cities, approved March twelfth, eighteen hundred and eighty.

In cities of this state where the office of president of the board of education, or board of directors of education exists, or is created by any general or special law, such president shall hereafter receive no salary or compensation whatever for performing the duties of such office, but nothing herein contained shall be deemed or taken to affect or take away the salary of the present incumbent of any such office.

Supplement passed March twenty-third, eighteen hundred and eighty-one.

No child to be excluded from any public school.

1. No child between the age of five and eighteen years of age shall be excluded from any public school in this state on account of his or her religion, nationality or color.

Penalty for board of trustees to vote to exclude any child from any public school.

2. Any member of any board of trustees of any school district, or any member of any board of education in this state, who shall vote to exclude from any public school in this state, any child between the age of five and eighteen years of age, on account of his or her religion, nationality or color, shall be deemed guilty of a misdemeanor, and on conviction thereof shall be punished by a fine of not less than fifty dollars, nor more than two hundred and fifty dollars, or by imprisonment in the county jail, work-house or penitentiary, of the county in which the offence is committed, not less than thirty days, nor more than six months, or both fine and imprisonment may be imposed in the discretion of the court.

AN ACT providing for the establishment of schools for industrial education, approved March twenty-fourth, eighteen hundred and eighty-one.

WHEREAS, The establishment of well conducted and liberally supported schools for the training and education of pupils in industrial and mechanical pursuits, must tend to supply a growing want in our community of skilled mechanics, artisans and agriculturists; *and whereas* it is especially the duty of the state to afford good educational facilities to its youth in those technical studies, which are directly associated with the material prosperity of its people; therefore, Preamble.

1. Whenever any board of education, school committee, or other like body, of any city, town, or township in this state, shall certify to the governor that a sum of money, not less than three thousand dollars, has been contributed by voluntary subscriptions of citizens, or otherwise, as hereinafter authorized, for the establishment in any such city, town or township, of a school or schools for industrial education, it shall be the duty of the said governor to cause to be drawn, by warrant of the comptroller, approved by himself, out of any moneys in the state treasury not otherwise appropriated, an amount equal to that contributed by the particular locality as aforesaid for the said object; and when any such school or schools shall have been established in any locality as aforesaid, there shall be annually contributed by the state, in manner aforesaid, for the maintenance and support thereof, a sum of money equal to that contributed each year in said locality for such purpose; *provided, however,* that the moneys contributed by the state, as aforesaid, to any locality shall not exceed in any one year the sum of five thousand dollars.

Governor authorized to draw amount of money equal to amount contributed for the establishment of schools for industrial education.

Proviso.

2. All moneys raised and contributed as aforesaid shall be applied under the direction of a board of trustees, organized as hereinafter provided, to the establishment and support of schools for the training and education of pupils in industrial pursuits (including agriculture), so as to

Moneys raised and contributed applied under direction of board of trustees.

enable them to perfect themselves in the several branches of industry, which require technical instruction.

Cities, towns and townships empowered to raise by tax sum for support of schools.

3. Any city, town or township, shall have power to appropriate and raise by tax for the support of any such school therein, such sum of money as they may deem expedient and just.

Board of trustees, how constituted.

4. There shall be a board of trustees of each of such schools, which shall consist of the governor, ex-officio, who shall be president thereof; two persons selected by the state board of education; two by citizens and associations contributing; two by the board of education, school committee or other like body of the locality where such school is established; and one by the common council, township committee or other governing body thereof, if such city, town or township shall contribute to the maintenance of such school; the said board of trustees shall have control of the buildings and grounds owned and used by such schools, the application of the funds for the support thereof, the regulation of the tuition fees, the appointment and removal of teachers, the power to prescribe the studies and exercises of the school and rules for its management, to grant certificates of graduation, to appoint some suitable person treasurer of the board, and to frame and modify at pleasure such by-laws as they may deem necessary for their own government; they shall report annually to the state and local boards of education their own doings and the progress and condition of the schools.

Board of trustees to have control of buildings, application of funds and general management of schools

Expenses of trustees, how paid.

5. The said trustees shall receive no compensation for their services, but the expenses necessarily incurred by them in the discharge of their duties shall be paid upon the approval of the governor.

BLANKS AND FORMS

FOR SCHOOL OFFICERS.

BLANKS AND FORMS FOR SCHOOL OFFICERS.

The following Forms have been prepared for the use of all officers having duties to discharge under the School Law. Their use will secure uniformity and correctness in the transaction of financial and general school business. The *literal* use of these Forms is in no case *essential* to the validity of a school instrument. Any Form may be used which clearly expresses the objects designed, or the intention of the parties interested, and conforms in all respects to the requirements of the law, but as those annexed have been prepared with strict reference to these necessary conditions, their use is recommended. The blank spaces are to be filled to meet the varying circumstances in each case. These Forms have been submitted to and approved by the State Board of Education.

ELLIS A. APGAR,
State Superintendent of Public Instruction.

BLANKS AND FORMS.

No. 1.—*Order for County Superintendent's Salary.*

No. ——. OFFICE OF STATE SUPERINTENDENT,
TRENTON, N. J., —— ——, 18——.

To the Collector of —— County:

Pay to the order of —— ——, County Superintendent of —— County, ——$\frac{}{100}$ Dollars, being the amount of salary due to —— ——, 18——.

$——. —— ——, *State Superintendent.*

No. 2.—*Order for County Superintendent's Expenses.*

No. ——. DEPARTMENT OF PUBLIC INSTRUCTION,
TRENTON, N. J., —— ——, 18——.

To the Collector of —— County:

Pay to the order of —— ——, County Superintendent of —— County, ——$\frac{}{100}$ Dollars, being the amount due for expenses incurred in the performance of his official duties from —— ——, 18——, to —— ——, 18——.

$——. —— ——, *State Superintendent.*

NOTE.—The amount for expenses cannot exceed $300.

No. 3.—*Order on Comptroller for the State Appropriation of $100,000.*

No. ———. DEPARTMENT OF PUBLIC INSTRUCTION,
TRENTON, N. J., ——— ——, 18——.

To the Comptroller of the State of New Jersey:

Pay to the order of the Collector of ——— County, ———$\frac{}{100}$ Dollars, being the amount apportioned for the support of Public Schools in said County, out of the State Appropriation of $100,000, for the School Year beginning Sept. 1st, 18——, and ending August 31st, 18——.

$———. ——— ———, *State Superintendent.*

No. 4.—*Order on the Comptroller for the State School Tax.*

No. ———. DEPARTMENT OF PUBLIC INSTRUCTION,
TRENTON, N. J., ——— ——, 18——.

To the Comptroller of the State of New Jersey:

Pay to the order of the Collector of ——— County, ———$\frac{}{100}$ Dollars, being the amount apportioned for the support of Public Schools in said County, out of the State School Tax, for the School Year beginning Sept. 1st, 18——, and ending August 31st, 18——.

$———. ——— ———, *State Superintendent.*

No. 5.—*Order on County Collector for State Appropriation of $100,000.*

No. ———. OFFICE OF COUNTY SUPERINTENDENT,
———, N. J., ——— ——, 18——.

To the Collector of ——— County:

Pay to the order of the Collector of ——— Township, ———$\frac{}{100}$ Dollars, being the amount apportioned out of the State Appropriation of $100,000, for the support of Public Schools in said County, for the School Year beginning Sept. 1st, 18——, and ending August 31st, 18——.

$———. ——— ———, *County Superintendent.*

No. 6.—*Order on County Collector for the State School Tax.*

No. ——. OFFICE OF COUNTY SUPERINTENDENT,
——, N. J., —— ——, 18——.

To the Collector of —— County:

Pay to the order of the Collector of —— Township, ——$\frac{}{100}$ Dollars, being the amount apportioned out of the State School Tax for the support of Public Schools in said County, for the School Year beginning Sept. 1st, 18——, and ending August 31st, 18——.

$——. —— ——, *County Superintendent.*

No. 7.—*Order on County Collector for the Interest of Surplus Revenue.*

No. ——. OFFICE OF COUNTY SUPERINTENDENT,
——, N. J., —— ——, 18——.

To the Collector of —— County:

Pay to the order of the Collector of —— Township, ——$\frac{}{100}$ Dollars, being the amount apportioned out of the Interest of the Surplus Revenue for the support of Public Schools in said County, for the School Year beginning Sept. 1st, 18——, and ending August 31st, 18——.

$——. —— ——, *County Superintendent.*

No. 8.—*Order for County Examiner's Salary.*

No. ——. OFFICE OF COUNTY SUPERINTENDENT,
——, N. J., —— ——, 18——.

To the Collector of —— County:

Pay to the order of —— ——, County Examiner, ——$\frac{}{100}$ Dollars, being the amount due him for services rendered at the —— session of the Board of County Examiners, and for traveling expenses, in accordance with Section 49 of the School Law.

$——. —— ——, *County Superintendent.*

No. 9.—*Application for State Aid to Establish a School Library.*

———, N. J., ——— ———, 18——.

To the State Superintendent of Public Instruction:

SIR:—We, the undersigned, Trustees of School District No. ———, of the Township of ———, County of ———, State of New Jersey, do hereby certify, that there has been raised in our District, by subscription [or entertainment, as the case may be], the sum of ——— Dollars, for the purpose of establishing a School Library within our District, in accordance with the provisions of Section 95 of the Revised School Law. And we therefore request you to send an order for the amount due us from the State in accordance with the further provisions of said act.

——— ———, *D. C.*
——— ———, } *Trustees.*
——— ———,

NOTE.—The first appropriation is twenty dollars, and subsequent ones ten dollars.

No. 10.—*Order for Library Appropriation.*

No. ———. DEPARTMENT OF PUBLIC INSTRUCTION,
TRENTON, N. J., ——— ———, 18——.

To the Comptroller of the State of New Jersey:

It having been certified to me that the sum of ——— Dollars has been raised by subscription [or entertainment, as the case may be], in District No. ———, of the County of ———, State of New Jersey, in accordance with the provisions of Section 95 of the Revised School Law, therefore you will pay to the order of ——— ———, District Clerk of said District, the sum of ——— Dollars, to be used only for the purposes specified in said act.

$———. ——— ———, *State Superintendent.*

No. 11.—*Order on Township Collector for Teacher's Salary.*

No. ——. ——, N. J., —— ——, 18——.

To —— ——, Township Collector for the Township of ——, County of ——, State of New Jersey:

Pay to the order of —— ——, Teacher, ——$\frac{}{100}$ Dollars, being the amount of Salary due —— for teaching our Public School from —— ——, 18——, to —— ——, 18——.

—— ——, *D. C.*
—— ——,
—— ——,
Trustees of District No. ——, County of ——.

I hereby certify that —— ——, the Teacher in whose favor this order is drawn, is in possession of a Teacher's Certificate, in full force and effect, and that —— has properly kept the School Register as required by law, and that I have certified thereto in said Register.

—— ——, *District Clerk.*

NOTE.—Money raised by district tax can be used for such school purposes as are specified at the meeting at which the money is ordered. All other school money, except twenty dollars annually, which the law allows for incidental expenses, must be reserved for the payment of teacher's salary and fuel bills.

Payments can only be made for the support of those schools that conform in all respects to the provisions of the School Law, and to those teachers only who possess certificates in full force and effect covering the time for which salary is demanded, and who have kept the School Register in the manner prescribed.

The Collector should invariably refuse to pay orders until he is satisfied that all these conditions have been complied with.

No. 12.—*Order on Township Collector for District School Tax raised for other purposes than the Payment of Teacher's Salary.*

To —— ——, Township Collector for the Township of ——, County of ——, State of New Jersey:

Pay to the order of —— ——, ——$\frac{}{100}$ Dollars, for [*here state for what the money is to be paid*] out of the funds raised by District School Tax in our District, now in your hands.

—— ——, *D. C.*
—— ——,
—— ——,
Trustees of District No. ——, County of ——.

No. 13.—*Financial Report of District Clerk to County Superintendent.*

To ——— ———, County Superintendent for ——— County:

Sir:—I herewith submit the Financial Report of School District No. ——, for the School Year ending August 31, 18——.

RECEIPTS.

Balance in hands of Collector August 31st, 18——, exclusive of that for building purposes..........................	$———
Balance in hands of Collector August 31st, 18——, for building and repairing	———
Apportionment from State Appropriation...	———
Apportionment from Township School Tax..................	———
Apportionment from Surplus Revenue.........................	———
Amount raised by District Tax for teachers' salaries, &c....	———
Amount raised by District Tax for building and repairing..	———
Amount received from other sources..........................	———
Total receipts..	———

EXPENDITURES.

Amount expended for Teachers' Wages	$———
Amount expended for Fuel..	———
Amount expended for Incidentals...............................	———
Amount expended for Building and Repairing School House..	———
Total expenditures.........	$———
Balance due the District..	$———

I certify that the foregoing statement is correct in all respects.

——— ———, *District Clerk.*

No. 14.—*Financial Report of District Clerk to Township Committee.*

To the Township Committee of ——— Township:

Sirs:—[*Form of Report same as No.* 13].

No. 15.—*Financial Report of District Clerk to the People of the District.*

To the Inhabitants of School District No. ——— :

[*Form of Report same as No.* 13].

Note.—The above report should be made at the annual school meeting held for the election of Trustees.

No. 16.—*Annual Report of Trustees to the District.*

To the Inhabitants of School District No. ——— :

In obedience to the requirements of the School Law, we beg leave to present our annual report for the past School Year [*here give the final report required of the Teacher in the School Register; state what has been done by the Trustees during the year; discuss school matters; make suggestions, etc., etc.*]

All of which is respectfully submitted.

——— ———, *D. C.*
——— ———,
——— ———,
} *Trustees of School District No.* ——.

Dated ——— ——, 18——.

Note.—The above report should be made at the annual school meeting for the election of Trustees.

No. 17.—*Report of District Clerk to County Superintendent of the Amount of District School Tax Ordered to be Raised.*

To the County Superintendent of ——— County:

Sir:—I hereby report to you, that at the annual (*or a special, as the case may be*) meeting of the legal voters of School District No. ——, of the County of ———, held on the ——— day of ———, 18——, there was voted to be raised [*write the amount in words*] dollars, as District School Tax, for the purpose of [*here state the object for which the money is to be used*].

——— ———, *District Clerk.*

No. 18.—*Report of Township Collector to County Superintendent of the Amount of Township School Tax Ordered to be Raised.*

To the County Superintendent of ——— County:

SIR:—I hereby report to you that the amount of School Tax voted to be raised in ——— Township at the last annual town meeting, held on the ——— day of ———, 18——, is [*write the amount in words*] Dollars per child [*or* ——— *Dollars, as the case may be*].

The Interest on Surplus Revenue to be apportioned to the Public Schools of this Township is ——— Dollars.

Dated this ——— day of ———, 18——.

——— ———, *Township Collector.*

NOTE.—This report should be sent to the County Superintendent within five days after the town meeting If the amount of interest on surplus revenue is not known at that time, a separate report should be made of that item as soon as the amount is ascertained. In some counties the surplus revenue remains as a county fund, and the amount of interest must be reported by the County Collector to the County Superintendent.

No. 19.—*Report of County Clerk to County Superintendent of the Names and Post Office Addresses of the Township Collectors and City Treasurers.*

To the County Superintendent of ——— County:

SIR:—I hereby report to you the names and addresses of the newly elected Township Collectors [*and City Treasurers if there be any*] of this County, as follows:

Names of Township or City.	Names of Collectors and City Treasurers.	Address.
....	....	
....	....	
....	....	
....	....	

——— ———, *County Clerk.*

No. 20.—*Financial Report of Township Collector to County Superintendent.*

———, N. J., ——— 18—.

To ———, County Superintendent for ——— County:

SIR:—I herewith submit the Financial Report for the School Districts of the Township of ———, for the School Year ending August 31st, 18—.

DISTRICTS.	Balance from Last Year.			Received from State Appropriation, including State School Tax.	Received from Township Tax.	Received from Surplus Revenue.	Received from District Tax.	Total receipts, including Balance.	Paid for Teachers' Salaries.	Paid for Fuel.	Paid for Incidentals.	Paid for Building and Repairs.	Total amount paid.	Balance of State, County, and Township Funds unexpended.	Balance of District Funds unexpended.
	Balance from State Fund, Surplus Revenue and Township Tax.	Balance from District Tax.	Total Balance.												
No.															

State of New Jersey, ——— County *ss.*

On this ——— day of ———, A. D. 18—, before me, personally came ——— ———, Township Collector of ——— Township, who made oath (or affirmation) that the above Financial Report is true to the best of his knowledge and belief.

NOTE.—The above report should be made to the County Superintendent, on or before the first day of September, and a duplicate sent to the Township Committee.

No. 21.—*Manner of Keeping the School Register.*

No. of Scholars	Names of Scholars.	YEARS OF AGE.	MONDAY.	TUESDAY.	WEDNESDAY.	THURSDAY.	FRIDAY.	MONDAY.	TUESDAY.	WEDNESDAY.	THURSDAY.	FRIDAY.	MONDAY.	TUESDAY.	WEDNESDAY.	THURSDAY.	FRIDAY.	MONDAY.	TUESDAY.	WEDNESDAY.	THURSDAY.	FRIDAY.	Number of Days attendance for four Weeks.	Number of Months attendance for twelve Weeks.	ALPHABET.	SPELLING.	READING.	WRITING.	GRAMMAR.	ARITHMETIC.	GEOGRAPHY	HISTORY
1	Andrew Jones,	6	X	X	X		Ẋ	X		X	∵	/	/	X	X	X	X	X	X		X	X	16		/							
2	Caleb Martin,	9	X	X	X	X	X	X	X	X	X	X	X	X	X	X	X	X	X	X	X	X	20			/	/	/		/	/	
3	John Smith,	15	X	X	X		X	X	X	∵	/		X	Ẋ	X	/	X	X	—	—	—	—	13			/	/	/	/	/		/
4	Susan Parker,	11	X		Ẋ	X	X	\	/	X	X	X	X	X		/	X	∵	X	X	X	X	16½			/	/	/		/	/	
5	Anna Mount,	7	X	X	X	X	/	X	X	X	X	X	X	X	—	—	—	—	—	—	—	—	11½			/	/					
6	David Case,	16	X	X	X	X	X	X	X	X	X	X	X	X	X	X	X	X	X	X	X	X	20			/	/	/	/	/		/
7	Francis Moore,	9	X	X	X	X	X	X	X		/	∵	X	X	/	Ẋ	/	/	X	X	X	X	17			/	/	/		/	/	
8	George Brown,	8	X	∵	/	Ẋ	X	\	\	X	/		X	X			/	/	X			X	12			/	/	/		/	/	
9	Julia Brown,	10	X	X	X	X	X		X	X		X	Ẋ	Ẋ	X	X				X	X	X	15			/	/	/		/	/	
10	Mary Case,	5	X	Ẋ	X	\		X	X	∵	/	X	X	X	X	X	X	X	X	X	X	X	18		/							
11	Sarah Cook,	13	—	—	—	—	—	—	—	—	X	X	X	X	X	X	X	X	X	X	X	X	12			/	/	/	/	/	/	/
		Number of Scholars in each of the above Studies..................																							2	9	9	8	3	8	6	3

I hereby Certify that the foregoing are true and correct statistics.

SILAS JONES,

Teacher.

Explanation of the manner of Keeping the School Register, as shown in the Model on the preceding page.

Indicates presence all day.

Indicates presence during the forenoon only.

Indicates presence during the afternoon only.

Indicates presence during the forenoon only, but tardy.

Indicates presence during the afternoon only, but tardy.

Indicates presence all day, but tardy in the forenoon.

Indicates presence all day, but tardy in the afternoon.

Indicates presence all day, but tardy both forenoon and afternoon.

Indicates absence all day.

If the scholar does not enter the School at the beginning of the term, a horizontal line is drawn to the day of entering. If the scholar, for any cause, leaves the School before the close of the term, a similar line is drawn from the day of his leaving.

In the blanks under the names of the branches taught, diagonal lines are drawn to indicate the several studies each scholar is pursuing.

No. 22.—*Teacher's Report to the County Superintendent when Leaving a School before the end of the School Year.*

Report of the Teacher of Public School ———, in District No. ———, in the County of ———, for the portion of the School Year commencing September 1st, 18——, and ending ——— ——, 18——.

[*The body of the Report same as No. 23.*]

To ——— ———, County Superintendent for ——— County:

Being about to leave my present School, I respectfully present the above record and statements as my report for the expired portion of the present School Year, as required by the laws of this State; which report I hereby certify has been carefully made out from the records contained in the School Register.

——— ———, *Teacher.*

NOTE.—The law requires that a duplicate of the above report shall be made to the District Clerk.

No. 23.—*Teacher's Annual Report to District Clerk and County Superintendent.*

Annual Report of the Teacher of Public School ——, in District No. ——, of the County of ——, for the Year commencing September 1, 18—, and ending August 31, 18—.

1	2	3	4	5	6	7	8	9	10	11	12	13	14	15	16	17	18	19	20	21	22	23	24
Number of months the School has been kept open during the year.	Number of children between five and eighteen years of age enrolled in the School Register during the year.	Number who have attended ten months, or more, during the year.	Number who have attended eight months, but less than ten.	Number who have attended six months, but less than eight.	Number who have attended four months, but less than six.	Number who have attended less than four months.	Average number who have attended School during the time it has been kept open.	Estimated number of children in the District attending Private Schools.	Estimated number of children in the District who have attended no School during the year	Number of children the School house will seat comfortably.	Number of pupils who have not been absent or tardy during the year.	Are the children required to study at home?	Is there uniformity of text-books?	How many studies are pursued in the room? (Different grades in same subject to be considered different studies)	Average number of recitations heard daily.	Average term enrollment.	Average daily attendance. (Answer same as for number 8).	Average number of cases of tardiness per day.	Percentage of daily attendance upon average term enrollment. (Divide 18 by 17).	Percentage of promptness upon average daily attendance. (Divide 19 by 18, and subtract from 100).	Number of children suspended or expelled during the year.	Number of visits by Trustees.	Grade of certificate held by Teacher.

To the District Clerk of School District No. ——, [*or to the County Superintendent, as the case may be.*]

I respectfully present the above record and statements as my final report for the past School Year, as required by the laws of this State; which report, I hereby certify, has been carefully made out from the records contained in the School Register.

—— ——, *Teacher.*

Note.—This report should be sent to the District Clerk and the County Superintendent at the time the School closes for the Summer vacation.

No. 24.—*Teacher's Quarterly Report to District Clerk.*

QUARTERLY REPORT of the Teacher of Public School, District No. ———, in the County of ———, for the quarter commencing ———, 18———, and ending ———, 18———.

To ——— ———, District Clerk :

Whole number of Girls Enrolled in the Register.	Whole number of Boys Enrolled in the Register.	Total Number Enrolled.	Number who have not been Absent during the twelve weeks.	Number who have attended eight weeks, but less than twelve.	Number who have attended four weeks but less than eight.	Number who have attended less than four weeks.	Average Daily Attendance.	Percentage of Attendance.	Number who have not been Tardy.	Number who are usually Tardy.	Number punished in any way.	Number Suspended or Expelled.	Number Studying the Alphabet.	Number Studying Spelling.	Number Studying Reading.	Number Studying Writing	Number Studying Grammar.	Number Studying Arithmetic.	Number Studying Geography.	Number Studying History.	Number Studying other branches.	Number of Different Classes under my Charge.

I respectfully present the above record and statements, as my report for the past quarter, which, I hereby certify, has been carefully made out from the records contained in the School Register.

——— ———, *Teacher.*

NOTE.—To ascertain the "average daily attendance," divide the aggregate number of days all the scholars together have attended during the quarter by the number of days the school has been in session, and the quotient will be the average attendance required.

To find the "percentage of attendance," add two ciphers to the average attendance, and divide the number by the "total number enrolled," and the quotient will be the percentage of attendance.

No. 25.—*Notice to County Superintendent of a Vacancy in Board of Trustees.*

To ——— ———, County Superintendent:

SIR:—You are hereby notified that a vacancy now exists in the Board of Trustees of School District No. ——, in the County of ———, through [*here state the cause of the vacancy*] which you are requested to fill by appointment.

Dated this ——— day of ———, 18——.

——— ———, *District Clerk.*

NOTE.—The above notice should be sent to the County Superintendent as soon as the vacancy exists. If the office of District Clerk is vacant, the notice should be sent by one of the other Trustees.

No. 26.—*Appointment to fill a Vacancy in a Board of Trustees.*

To ——— ———:

The office of one of the Trustees of School District No. ——, in the County of ———, having become vacant through failure of the District to elect according to law [*or for any other reason*], you are hereby appointed to fill such vacancy until the next annual meeting for the election of Trustees in said District.

Dated this ——— day of ———, 18——.

——— ———, *County Superintendent.*

No. 27.—*Appointment of a District Clerk.*

To ——— ———:

The office of District Clerk of School District No. ——, in the County of ———, being vacant through failure of the Trustees to elect according to law [*or for any other reason*], you are hereby appointed to fill such vacancy until the next annual meeting for the election of Trustees in said District.

Dated this ——— day of ———, 18——.

——— ———, *County Superintendent.*

No. 28.—*Appointment of Trustees for a New District.*

To ——— ———:

Having, on the ——— day of ———, 18———, formed a new School District, to be known as School District No. ———, in the County of ———, comprising the following territory: [*here insert the description of the District*] you are hereby appointed Trustee [*and District Clerk, if such is the fact,*] for said District until the next annual meeting for the election of Trustees.

I have appointed as your associates, Messrs. ——— ——— and ——— ———.

Dated this ——— day of ———, 18———.

——— ———, *County Superintendent.*

NOTE.—Where two Districts are united they each become extinct and a new District is formed, and the Trustees of the extinct Districts cannot continue to act as Trustees of the new one, but an entire new Board must be appointed by the County Superintendent.

No. 29.—*Request for District Clerk to Call a Special School Meeting for Establishing a Graded School.*

To ——— ———, District Clerk of School District No. ———, in the County of ———:

SIR:—You are hereby requested to call a special meeting of the legal voters of your District, on the ——— day of ———, 18———, at ——— o'clock in the ———noon, for the purpose of acting upon the question of uniting with Districts Nos. ——— and ———, etc., in establishing and maintaining a Graded School in accordance with the provisions of Section 61 of the School Law.

Dated this ——— day of ———, 18———.

——— ———, *County Superintendent.*

NOTE.—The above request is only to be given when there is a known desire on the part of the inhabitants of the Districts thus notified to establish a Graded School. A separate meeting should be held in each District proposing to unite.

No. 30.—*Notice for a Special District Meeting for Considering the Question of Establishing a Graded School.*

Notice is hereby given to the legal voters of School District No. ———, in the County of ———, that a special school meeting will be held at ———, on the ——— day of ———, 18———, at ——— o'clock in the ———noon, for the purpose of considering the question of uniting with Districts Nos. ——— and ———, etc., in establishing and maintaining a Graded School, in accordance with the provisions of Section 61 of the School Law.

Dated this ——— day of ———, 18———.

——— ———, *District Clerk.*

By order of ——— ———, *County Superintendent.*

NOTE—The above notice must be made conspicuous in several places, and posted ten days previous to the time of the meeting. The Districts separately, in accordance with the provisions of Section 86 can vote for, and cause to be assessed, a district tax for erecting the School building, or maintaining the School.

No. 31.—*Notice to County Superintendent, giving the result of the action of a School Meeting called for the purpose of Establishing a Graded School.*

To ———, County Superintendent of ——— County:

SIR:—At a meeting of the legal voters of School District No. ———, in the County of ———, held on the ——— day of ———, 18———, which was called pursuant to your order, the question of uniting with Districts Nos. ——— and ———, for the purpose of establishing a Graded School, was decided in the ———; ——— voting in the affirmative, and ——— in the negative.

Dated this ——— day of ———, 18———.

——— ———, *District Clerk.*

No. 32.—*Order organizing a Union School District for the purpose of Establishing a Graded School.*

WHEREAS, Districts now known as School Districts, Nos.———, ——— and ———, in the County of ———, did, in accordance with the provisions of Section 61 of the School Law, agree to unite, for the purpose of establishing and maintaining a Graded School, at public meetings called by order of the County Superintendent, on the following days, to wit: School District No. ——— on the ——— day of ———, 18———; School District No. ——— on the——— day of ———, 18———; and School District No.——— on the ——— day of ———, 18———.

Therefore, it is hereby ordered and made known that said districts are united for the purposes set forth, to be known hereafter by the name and title of ———.

Given under my hand this ——— day of ———, 18———.

——— ———, *County Superintendent.*

NOTE.—One copy of the above order must be furnished to each Board of Trustees of the United District, and one copy retained by the County Superintendent.

No. 33.—*Order Organizing a School District.*

It is hereby ordered and determined that the following shall hereafter be the boundaries of School District, to be known as District Number ———, in the County of ———, State of New Jersey: beginning at [*here describe the boundaries.*]

Given under my hand this ——— day of ———, 18———.

——— ———, *County Superintendent.*

Approved this ——— day of ———, 18———.

——— ———, *Secretary of State Board.*

NOTE.—The above order should be made out in duplicate, one copy to be retained by the County Superintendent, in his office, and the other to be held by the Trustees. The State Board prescribes that a map of the Districts of the County shall be drawn by the County Superintendent, and sent to the State Superintendent, to be retained in his office.

No. 34.—*Order altering the Boundaries of a School District.*

It is hereby ordered and determined that the [*here describe the territory by sections and parts of sections*], now a part of School District No. ———, in the County of ———, is taken from said District and attached to and made a part of School District No. ———, in said County, for all School purposes whatsoever.

This order will take effect on the ——— day of ———, 18———.

Given under my hand this ——— day of ———, 18———.

——— ———, *County Superintendent.*

Approved this — day of ———, 18———.

——— ———, *Secretary of State Board.*

No. 35.—*Notice by County Superintendent to the District Clerks of Districts to be affected by proposed District changes.*

To ——— ———, District Clerk of School District No. ———, in the County of ———:

You are hereby notified that I will be present at ———, on the ———day of ———, 18———, ——— o'clock in the ———noon, to decide upon certain proposed alterations of the boundaries of your School District. The attendance of your Board of Trustees is requested.

Dated this ——— day of ———, 18———.

——— ———, *County Superintendent.*

No. 36.—*Notice of Meeting of Township Board of Trustees.*

You are hereby notified that I will be present at ———, on the ——— day of ———, 18———, at ——— o'clock in the ——— noon, to meet "The Township Board of Trustees" of ——— Township. The attendance of your Board of Trustees is requested.

Dated this ——— day of ———, 18———.

——— ———, *County Superintendent.*

No. 37.—*Township Collector's Account with Districts.*

School District No. ——, of the County of ——, N. J.

RECEIPTS.						EXPENDITURES.				
Date.		Dolls.	Cts	Dolls	Cts.	Date	In Whose Favor Drawn.	For What Purpose.	Dolls.	Cts.
1881. Sept. 1.	Balance of last year from State Appropriation—Surplus Revenue and Township School Tax									
"	Balance of last year from District School Tax									
	Total Amount of Balance									
	Amount received from State									
	" " " "									
	" " " "									
	" " " Surplus Revenue									
	" " " Township School Tax									
	" " " District School Tax									
	Total Amount of Receipts									
	Total Balance and Receipts									
1882. Aug. 31.	Unexpended Balance from State Appropriation—Surplus Revenue and Township School Tax									
"	Unexpended Balance from District School Tax									
	Total Amount of Balance due District August 31, 1881									

Note.—Each District Clerk should also keep an account of the finances of his own District in a manner similar to the above.

No. 38.—*Notice to Township Collector, directing him to withhold School Moneys from a Teacher.*

To the Township Collector of ——— Township:

SIR:—You are hereby directed to withhold all further payment of salary to ——— ———, a teacher now employed in School District No. ——, situated in your Township, said teacher not being in possession of a certificate [*or not having kept the School Register*], as is required by the School Law.

Dated this ——— day of ———, 18——.

——— ———, *County Superintendent.*

No. 39.—*Notice to Township Collector, directing him to withhold School Moneys from a District.*

To the Township Collector of ——— Township:

SIR:—You are hereby directed to withhold [*here state the amount in words*] from the school moneys apportioned to School District No. ——, situated in your Township, on account of said District, [*here state the reason why the money is withheld*].

Dated this ——— day of ———, 18——.

——— ———, *County Superintendent.*

NOTE.—All moneys withheld must be reapportioned the next year among all the Districts of the Township.

No. 40.—*Notice of Meeting for Examination of Teachers.*

Notice is hereby given that there will be a meeting of the County Board of Examiners of ——— County, for the examination of candidates for teachers' certificates, at ———, on ———, the ——— instant. Each applicant for a certificate should be present as early as ——— o'clock, A. M.

——— ———, *County Superintendent.*

——— ———, 18——

No. 41.—*Notice to Teacher Revoking his Certificate.*

To ——— ———:

SIR:—The certificate of qualification held by you as a Public School Teacher in the County of ———, issued on the ——— day of ———, 18——, is hereby revoked, for the reason that [*here state reason why certificate is revoked*].

Dated this ——— day of ———, 18——.

——— ———, *County Superintendent.*

NOTE.—In cases where the teacher's offence is not flagrant, and the certificate revoked is freely surrendered on request of the Superintendent, none but the parties immediately concerned need be apprised of the transaction. But if the teacher refuses to deliver up his certificate, public notice of the revocation should be made in the papers. All revocations of State certificates and County certificates of the first grade must be made by the State Superintendent.

No. 42.—*Notice to District Clerk informing him of the Revocation of Teacher's Certificate.*

To ——— ———, District Clerk of School District No. ———, of the County of ———:

SIR:—You are hereby notified that on the ——— day of ———, 18——, I revoked the certificate of qualification held by ——— ———, a teacher in your District, for the reason that, in my opinion, the said ——— ——— does not possess the requisite qualifications as a teacher in respect to [*moral character, learning, or ability to teach, as the case may be*].

Dated this ——— day of ———, 18——.

——— ———, *County Superintendent.*

NOTE.—When a teacher's certificate is revoked, a notice similar to the above should also be sent the Collector of the Township in which the teacher has been engaged.

No. 43.—*Notice by County Superintendent of Apportionment of School Money.*

OFFICE OF COUNTY SUPERINTENDENT,
——, N. J., —— ——, 18——.

Apportionment of School Moneys for the County of ——, for the School Year commencing September 1, 18——.

Amount of State School Tax appropriated by the State, $ ——

Additional State Appropriation, ... ——

Interest of Surplus Revenue, ... ——

Amount of Township School Tax, . . . ——

Amount of District School Tax, ... ——

Number of Children according to Census of 18——. . ——

TOWNSHIPS.	Districts, Name and Number.	Number of Children according to Census of 18——.	State School Tax.	State Appropriation.	Interest of Surplus Revenue.	Township School Tax.	District School Tax.	Total.
....	....	....	....	....	....	....	....	....
	....	....	....	....	....	....	....	....
	....	....	....	....	....	....	....	....
	....	....	....	....	....	....	....	....
	Total......	....	....	....	....	....	....	....
....	....	....	....	....	....	....	....	....
	....	....	....	....	....	....	....	....
	....	....	....	....	....	....	....	....
	....	....	....	....	....	....	....	....
	....	....	....	....	....	....	....	....
	Total......	....	....	....	....	....	....	....
	....	....	....	....	....	....	....	....
....	....	....	....	....	....	....	....	....
	....	....	....	....	....	....	....	....
	Total......	....	....	....	....	....	....	....

SUMMARY BY TOWNSHIPS.

....	....	....	....	....	....	....	....	....
....	....	....	....	....	....	....	....	....
....	....	....	....	....	....	....	....	....
Total for the County....	....	....	....	....	....	....	....	....

—— ——, *County Superintendent.*

NOTE.—Copy of the above should be furnished the County Collector, each Township Collector and each District Clerk.

No. 44.—*Notice for Annual Meeting for the Election of Trustees.*

Notice is hereby given to the legal voters of School District No. ———, in the County of ———, that the annual school meeting for the election of School Trustees will be held at ———, on Monday, the ——— day of ———, 18——, at ——— o'clock —— M.

Dated this ——— day of ———, 18——.

——— ———, *District Clerk.*

NOTE.—The above notice must be posted in three public places in the District, one of which shall be at the school house at least five days previous to the time of the meeting. The meeting must be held in the school house, if there is one.

No. 45.—*Notice for a Meeting of the District Board of Trustees.*

To ——— ———:

You are hereby notified that there will be a meeting of the Board of Trustees of School District No. ———, on ——— evening, ——— ———, 18——, at ——— o'clock, in the school house.

[*Date.*] ——— ——— *District Clerk.*

No. 46.—*Notice by District Clerk to County Superintendent of the Election of Trustees.*

To ——— ———, County Superintendent:

SIR:—You are hereby notified that at the annual meeting in School District No. ———, in the County of ———, held on the ——— day of ———, 18——, ——— ——— was elected Trustee in the place of ——— ———, whose term had expired.

The Board of Trustees now consists of

Mr. ——— ———, whose term expires 18——.
" ——— ———, " " " 18——.
" ——— ———, " " " 18——.

The Trustees have elected Mr. ——— ———, District Clerk, whose post office address is ———.

——— ———, *Secretary of School Meeting.*

NOTE.—This notice should be sent to the County Superintendent as soon after the election as possible. It may be sent by the District Clerk or the Secretary.

No. 47.—*Notice to be given by the Secretary of a District School Meeting, to the Officers Elect.*

To ——— ———:

You are hereby notified that at a meeting of School District No. ———, in the County of ———, held on the ——— day of ———, 18———, you were elected Secretary of said District.

Dated this day of ———, 18———.

——— ———, *Secretary of said Meeting.*

No. 48.—*Form of Resignation.*

To ——— ———, County Superintendent:

I hereby resign my office of Trustee [*or District Clerk*] of School District No. ———, in the County of ———.

Dated this ——— day of ———, 18———.

——— ———.

No. 49.—*Notice for the Annual District Meeting for determining what District School Tax shall be assessed.*

Notice is hereby given to the legal voters of School District No. ———, in the County of ———, that the annual school meeting will be held at ———, on the Tuesday of the week following town meeting, being the ——— day of March (or April), 18———, at ——— o'clock in the ——— noon, at which meeting will be submitted the question of voting a tax to maintain a free Public School the coming year [*or to build a school house, etc*].

The amount thought to be necessary for this purpose is ——— dollars.

Dated this ——— day of ———, 18———.

——— ———, *District Clerk.*

Note.—In the above notice must be particularly specified each item of business to be acted upon. For details, see Section 86, of the School Law.

No. 50.—*Notice for a Special District Meeting for determining what District School Tax shall be assessed.*

Notice is hereby given to the legal voters of School District No. ———, in the County of ———, that a special school meeting will be held at ———, on the ——— day of ———, 18———, at ——— o'clock in the ———noon, at which meeting will be submitted the question of ordering a district school tax to [*here particularly specify each item of business to be acted upon*].

The amount thought to be necessary for this purpose is ——— dollars.

——— ———, } *Trustees of*
——— ———, } *School District*
——— ———, } *No.* ———.

NOTE.—The authority for calling a special school meeting is given in Clause XI. of Section 39 of the School Law. For detailed directions, see Section 86.

No. 51.—*Various Specifications of Business to be Transacted that may be Inserted in any Notice for District Meeting, as they may be needed.*

To authorize the Trustees to purchase land and to erect a school house thereon;

To see if the District will take measures for the repair, alteration, enlarging or furnishing of the present school house;

To appoint a committee to prepare and report a plan for such erection or repair, with the probable expense of the same;

To raise money by district tax to defray the expenses of such erection, alteration or repair;

To authorize the Trustees to borrow money to defray the expenses of such erection, alteration or repair, and to provide for the payment of the same by ordering a district tax, [or by bonding the district, as the case may be];

To see if the District will vote a sufficient district tax to defray the expenses of maintaining a free School during the ensuing year, or during ——— months of the ensuing year; or the issuing of bonds;

To order a district tax for the payment of a debt of ——— dollars, now resting upon the school house property;

To order the sale of the present school house property, and to decide what disposition shall be made of the proceeds;

To do any other business within the scope of the foregoing propositions.

No. 52.—*Certificate of the amount of School Tax voted to be raised at a regular School Meeting in a School District, to be delivered by the District Clerk to the Township Assessor.*

To ———, Assessor of - —— Township, ——— County, State of New Jersey:

The legal voters of School District No. ——, in the County of ———-, met at ———, a convenient public place within the District, on the ——— day of ———, 18——, being the Tuesday of the week following the annual town meeting, to determine what additional school tax, if any, should be levied upon the District, and notice thereof, setting forth the time, place and object of said meeting, and specifying ——— dollars as the amount of money thought necessary to be raised, was given by the District Clerk, and set up at three public places within the District, ten days before the meeting; and the said legal voters, so met, by the consent of a majority of those present, authorized the Trustees of said District [*to purchase land, etc., as the case may be*], and ordered by a like vote ——— dollars for the purpose of [*as purchasing land*], and ——— dollars for the purpose of [*as building a school house*], etc., amounting in all to ——— dollars, which sum is not in excess of the amount thought to be necessary, as set forth in the notices, and you are therefore directed to assess the said sum of ——— dollars on the inhabitants of said School District, and their estates, and the taxable property therein, pursuant to the statute in such case made and provided.

Dated this ——— day of ———,. 18——.

——— ———, *District Clerk.*

State of New Jersey, } *ss.*
County of ——— }

———, being duly sworn on his oath, saith that he is the District Clerk of School District No. ——, in the County of ———, and that the above statement by him is correct and true.

Sworn and subscribed before me this ——— day of ———, 18——. ——— ———.

No. 53.—*Certificate of the Amount of School Tax voted to be raised at a Special School Meeting in a School District, to be delivered by the District Clerk to the Township Assessor.*

To ——, Assessor of —— Township, —— County, State of New Jersey:

Pursuant to a resolution passed at a meeting of the Trustees of School District No. ——, in the County of ——, held on the —— day of ——, 18——, as authorized by Subdivision 11 of Section 39 of the School Law, the legal voters of said District met at ——, a convenient place within the District, on the —— day of ——, 18——, to determine [*balance of form, including the affidavit, same as form No.* 52].

Notes to Forms Nos. 52 and 53.—The certificate must state which of the object or objects specified in Section 86, for which the money is raised. 3 Vr. 444. If more than one object is specified, the amount of money apportioned to each must be stated. 7 Vr. 89.

The law requires that notice of the above action should also be sent to the County Superintendent.

No. 54.—*Warrant of the Amount of School Tax to be raised to meet maturing bonds and accruing interest, to be delivered by the District Clerk to the Township Assessor.*

To ——, Assessor of —— Township, —— County, State of New Jersey:

You are hereby directed to assess on the inhabitants of School District No. ——, of the County of ——, and their estates and the taxable property therein, —— dollars, being —— dollars to meet Bond No. ——, falling due on the —— day of ——, 18——, and —— dollars to meet accruing interest on Bonds Nos. ——, ——, ——, issued by the Trustees of said District, as authorized by the legal voters at a meeting held on the —— day of ——, 18——, in conformity to the provisions of *Section eighty six of the School Law,* (*or, as the case may be, at the call of the Trustees, as provided in the eleventh division of the thirty-ninth section of the School Law.*)

Dated this —— day of ——, 18——.

[L. S.]

—— ——, }
—— ——, } *Trustees of School District No.* ——.
—— ——, }

Attest, —— ——, *District Clerk.*

No. 55.—*Teachers' County Certificate—First Grade.*

TEACHER'S CERTIFICATE.

OFFICE OF
COUNTY SUPERINTENDENT.

—— COUNTY,
STATE OF NEW JERSEY.

First Grade.

GRADE IN

Orthography ....
Reading..............................
Writing ....
Geography ....
Practical Arithmetic................
English Grammar....................
History of the United States......
Book-keeping ....
Theo'y and Practice of Teaching..
Physiology ....
Natural Philosophy.................
English Composition...............

....

having presented satisfactory evidence of good moral character, and having passed the required examination, with the results indicated in the annexed Grade, is hereby licensed as a Teacher in the Public Schools of this county for the term of five years from date, unless this certificate is sooner revoked.

GRADE IN

Algebra ....
Constitution of the United States..
School Law of New Jersey.........
General Average...................

SPECIAL CREDIT MARKS.

Music.................................
Drawing..............................
Elocution. ....
Gymnastics..........................
General appearance of examination papers.........................
Has taught—   years............

Given under our hands this —— day of ——, 18——.

—— ——,
—— ——, } *Examiners.*

—— ——, *County Superintendent.*

NOTE.—This certificate entitles the holder to teach in any County in the State.

No. 56.—*Teachers' County Certificate—Second Grade.*

TEACHER'S CERTIFICATE.

OFFICE OF
COUNTY SUPERINTENDENT.

——— COUNTY,
STATE OF NEW JERSEY,

Second Grade.

GRADE IN

Orthography ....
Reading ....
Writing ....
Geography ....
Practical Arithmetic..................
English Grammar.......................
History of the United States......
Book-keeping..........................
Theo'y and Practice of Teaching
General Average.....................

....

having presented satisfactory evidence of good moral character, and having passed the required examination, with the results indicated in the annexed Grade, is hereby licensed as a Teacher in the Public Schools of this county for the term of three years from date, unless this certificate is sooner revoked.

SPECIAL CREDIT MARKS.

Music ....
Drawing.................................
Elocution ....
Gymnastics ....
General appearance of examination papers.........................
Has taught ——— years...........

Given under our hands this ——— day of ———, 18——.

——— ———,
——— ———, } *Examiners.*

——— ———, *County Superintendent.*

No. 57.—*Teachers' County Certificate—Third Grade.*

TEACHER'S CERTIFICATE.

OFFICE OF
COUNTY SUPERINTENDENT.

——— COUNTY,
STATE OF NEW JERSEY.

Third Grade.

GRADE IN	
Orthography	....
Reading	....
Writing	....
Geography	....
Practical Arithmetic	....
English Grammar	....
General Average	....

....
having presented satisfactory evidence of good moral character, and having passed the required examination, with the results indicated in the annexed Grade, is hereby licensed as a Teacher in the Public Schools of this County for the term of one year from date, unless this certificate is sooner revoked.

SPECIAL CREDIT MARKS.	
Music	....
Drawing	....
Elocution	....
Gymnastics	....
General appearance of examination papers	....
Has taught ——— years	....

Given under our hands this ——— day of ———, 18——.

——— ———,
——— ———, } *Examiners.*

——— ———, *County Superintendent.*

No. 58.—*Teacher's State Certificate—First Grade.*

State of New Jersey,
Department of Public Instruction,
Superintendent's Office.

STATE CERTIFICATE.

First Grade.

The eminent qualifications and distinguished success of ——— ———, as a *Teacher*, having been established by thorough examination and satisfactory testimonials, ——— is hereby duly authorized to teach in any part of this State.

Done at the City of Trenton, this ——— day of ———, in the year of our Lord one thousand eight hundred and eighty ——, under the authority conferred by Section 48 of the Revised School Law.

——— ———, *State Superintendent of Public Instruction.*
——— ———, *Principal of the State Normal School.*

No. 59.—*Teacher's State Certificate—Second Grade.*

State of New Jersey,
Department of Public Instruction,
Superintendent's Office.

STATE CERTIFICATE.

Second Grade.

——— ——— having presented satisfactory evidence of good moral character, and having passed the required examination, is hereby Licensed as a Teacher in the Public Schools of this State for the term of Ten Years from date, unless this certificate is sooner revoked.

Given under our hands and seals this ——— day of ———, 18——.

——— ———, *State Superintendent of Public Instruction.*
——— ———, *Principal of the State Normal School.*

No. 60.—*Teacher's State Certificate—Third Grade.*

STATE OF NEW JERSEY,
DEPARTMENT OF PUBLIC INSTRUCTION,
SUPERINTENDENT'S OFFICE.

STATE CERTIFICATE.

Third Grade.

——— ———, having presented satisfactory evidence of good moral character, and having passed the required examination, is hereby LICENSED AS A TEACHER in the Public Schools of this State for the term of SEVEN YEARS from date, unless this certificate is sooner revoked.

Given under our hands and seals this ——— day of ———, 18——.

——— ———, *State Superintendent of Public Instruction.*
——— ———, *Principal of the State Normal School.*

No. 61.—*Certificate of County Superintendent in Appeals.*

OFFICE OF COUNTY SUPERINTENDENT,
———, N. J., ——— ———, 18——.

To ——— ———, State Superintendent of Public Instruction :

SIR :—I transmit, herewith, a full and correct statement of the facts, and the documentary evidence presented to me, in the case of ——— *vs.* ———, together with my decision thereon, from which appeal has been taken to the State Department.

I certify that the accompanying statement is correct to the best of my knowledge and belief.

——— ———, *County Superintendent for ——— County.*

NOTE.—The above certificate should be furnished by the County Superintendent in cases of appeals, when requested by the State Superintendent.

No. 62.—*Appeal to the State Superintendent.*

——, N. J., —— ——, 18——.

To —— ——, State Superintendent of Public Instruction:

SIR:—We herewith transmit a full and correct statement of the facts in the case of —— *vs.* ——, together with the decision of the County Superintendent thereon, from which decision we respectfully appeal for the following reasons: [*here state the reasons for making the appeal*].

We certify that the accompanying statements, together with the decision of the County Superintendent, are true to the best of our knowledge and belief.

—— ——,
—— ——.

No. 63.—*Form of Certificate Condemning a School House.*

This is to certify that we, the undersigned, have this day condemned the public school house in District No. ——, in the County of ——, as being, in its present condition, unfit for use.

Dated this —— day of ——, 18——.

—— ——, *County Superintendent.*

—— ——, } *Trustees of District No.* ——,
—— ——, } *in the County of* ——.

NOTE.—This certificate is held by the County Superintendent, and the school house remains condemned until repaired or rebuilt.

No. 64.—*Teacher's Report of the Suspension of a Pupil to the Trustees.*

To —— ——, District Clerk of School District No. ——, of the County of ——:

SIR:—You are hereby notified that I have this day suspended from my school ——, for [*here state the cause for suspension*].

Dated this —— day of ——, 18——.

—— ——, *Teacher.*

NOTE.—The School Law requires every suspension to be reported to the Trustees.

No. 65.—*Order of Business at a District School Meeting.*

1. Choose a Chairman and Secretary.
2. Read the notice calling the meeting.
3. Report of District Clerk.
4. Transaction of the business for which the meeting was called, as set forth in the notices.
5. Miscellaneous business.
6. Adjournment.

No. 66.—*Minutes of District School Meeting for the Election of Trustees.*

——, N. J., —— ——, 18——.

Pursuant to the following notice [*here copy the notice given*], the legal voters of School District No. —— convened at the school house and selected —— ——, Chairman, and —— ——, Secretary.

The Secretary read the notice of the meeting.

Mr. —— ——, District Clerk, presented the annual report of the Trustees, which was accepted.

On motion of Mr. —— ——, the meeting proceeded to elect a Trustee by ballot in the place of Mr. —— ——, whose term has expired. Mr. —— —— received a majority of all the votes cast, and was declared by the Chairman duly elected Trustee for the term of three years.

The District Clerk stated that there was a vacancy in the Board on account of the expiration of the term of appointment of Mr. —— ——, who, during the past year, had been appointed Trustee by the County Superintendent to fill the vacancy caused by the resignation of Mr. —— ——. The meeting again proceeded to ballot and Mr. —— —— was elected Trustee for the unexpired term of Mr. —— ——.

On motion of Mr. —— —— the meeting adjourned.

—— ——, *Secretary.*

No. 67.—*Minutes of Trustee Meeting.*

Pursuant to notice given to each member, the Board of Trustees of District No. 1, met in the school house on Monday evening, January 3, 1881. There were present, Messrs. James Fisk, Henry Jones, and Alpheus Taylor.

Henry Jones presided.

The applications of H. W. Clark, Edward Davis, and E. H. Long for the position of teacher in our public school were received.

After considerable discussion relative to the qualifications of each, the position was awarded to Edward Davis at a salary of one hundred dollars per month.

The District Clerk was instructed to inform Mr. Davis of his election, and request him to enter upon his duties on Monday, January 10, 1881.

The following bills were presented by the District Clerk, and ordered paid out of the funds raised by district tax:

E. H. Jackson, four tons of coal, @ $5.00 . . .	$20 00
W. J. Hopkins, one cord of wood, ...	8 00
Jane Gibson, cleaning school house, ...	5 00

It was ordered that the District Clerk procure two slate blackboards, each three feet by four feet, for the use of the school.

Adjourned.

ALPHEUS TAYLOR, *District Clerk.*

No. 68.—*Certificate to be attached to proceedings of a District Meeting by the person acting as Secretary.*

I hereby certify that the foregoing is a correct and complete record of the proceedings of [*the annual or special school meeting, as the case may be*], held in School District No. ———, in the County of ———, on the ——— day of ———, 18——.

——— ———, *Secretary.*

NOTE.—When the District Clerk is absent, or when he does not act as Secretary of the school meeting, the above certificate should be attached to the account of the proceedings before it is delivered to said Clerk.

No. 69.—*Minutes of District School Meeting for raising District Tax.*

———, N. J., ——— ———, 18——.

Pursuant to the following notice [*here copy the notice given*], the legal voters of School District No. ——, convened at the school house; ——— ——— was elected Chairman and ——— ——— Secretary of the meeting.

The Chairman stated the object of the meeting and read the notice which had been given.

Mr. ——— ——— moved that a district school tax of three hundred dollars be voted for the purpose of maintaining a free school ten months during the year. Mr. ——— ——— moved to amend by striking out "three hundred" and inserting "four hundred," which was agreed to, and the motion as amended was decided in the affirmative; ——— ——— voting in the affirmative, and ——— ——— in the negative.

Mr. ——— ——— moved that a district school tax of one hundred dollars be voted for the purpose of painting the school house. Mr. ——— ——— moved to amend by striking out "one hundred" and inserting "fifty," which motion was lost. The original motion was then agreed to; ——— ——— voting in the affirmative, and ——— ——— in the negative.

On motion of Mr. ——— ———, the meeting adjourned.

——— ———, *Chairman.*

——— ———, *Secretary.*

No. 70.—*Minutes of District School Meeting Ordering a New School House Erected.*

[*Commence as in preceding form.*]

The following business was transacted:

It was, upon motion, *Resolved*, That the comfort of the children and the best interest of the District, demand the erection of a new school house.

It was voted that D. S——— and P. V——— be appointed a

committee to prepare and report a plan for such new school house, with an estimate of the probable expense of the same, and report thereon at the next meeting.

It was voted that when this meeting adjourn it adjourn to meet again on the ——— day of ———, 18——, at ——— o'clock P. M.

The Trustees were directed to give the required ten days' notice of the adjourned meeting, and to set forth that the object of said meeting would be the consideration of the report of the committee in relation to the new school house and the ordering of the necessary district tax for the erection of the same.

On motion the meeting adjourned, etc.

ADJOURNED MEETING.

[*Commence in a manner similar to No.* 69.]

D. S——— and P. V———, the committee appointed therefor, made their report of a plan for a school house, together with an estimate of the expense of construction, which report was accepted and ordered to be recorded, and is in the words and figures following:

[*Here insert report.*]

After consideration and discussion of said report, it was voted that the same be adopted, and that the Trustees be directed to proceed in the erection of a house in accordance with such plan.

It was voted that a district tax of ——— dollars be assessed and collected to defray the expense of such school house, ——— voting in the affirmative, and ——— in the negative.

NOTE.—The foregoing form of minutes are given for the inexperienced. Those who are familiar with such duties may adopt or vary them as may seem best. The essential point is, to have the proceedings of district meetings *accurately recorded.* Much depends upon the minutes of these meetings, and hence they should be correctly kept and carefully preserved.

No. 71.—*Minutes of District School Meeting, Ordering the Bonding of the District.*

——, N. J., —— ——, 18——.

Pursuant to the following notice [*here copy the notice given*], the legal voters of School District No. ——, of the County of ——, convened at the school house. —— —— was elected Chairman, and —— ——, Secretary of the meeting.

The Chairman stated the object of the meeting, and read the notice that had been given.

The plans for a brick school house were submitted and explained by the Trustees, as authorized at a meeting held —— ——, 18——. The Trustees stated that the probable cost of the building would be four thousand dollars, and that five hundred dollars would be required to furnish the same, and to fence and grade the grounds.

The Trustees further stated that the lot, containing half-an-acre of ground, belonging to —— ——, and situated on the corner of —— and —— streets, could be purchased for five hundred dollars. This, in the judgment of the Trustees, was considered a desirable site for the new building.

On motion of —— ——, the following resolutions were adopted:

1. *Resolved,* That the lot for school purposes, recommended by the Trustees, be purchased.

2. *Resolved,* That a school house be erected thereon, in accordance with the plans and specifications submitted.

3. *Resolved,* That for the purpose of securing the money needed to purchase the lot, and to fence the same, and to erect and furnish the school house, the sum of five thousand dollars be raised by issuing five bonds of the District, in the corporate name of the District, in denominations of one thousand dollars each.

4. *Resolved,* That one bond shall be issued for one year; one for two years; one for three years; one for four years, and one for five years, and that each year, until the last bond is paid, a tax shall be levied, according to law, on the property and the inhabitants of the District, sufficient to pay the bond maturing, together with the accrued interest on all those then outstanding.

5. *Resolved,* That the Trustees be empowered to carry out the provisions of the foregoing resolutions.

The vote on the resolutions stood —— in the affirmative, and —— in the negative.

No. 72.—*Report of Non-Attendance of Children at School.*

To ——— ———, Township Collector:

You are hereby notified that the following children, between eight and fourteen years of age, residing in this District, have not attended school during the past year the time required by the act relative to the attendance of children at school, approved April 9th, 1875:

——— ——— has attended but ——— months.
——— ——— " " " ——— "
——— ——— " " " ——— "

You are requested to impose the penalty and to collect the fine, as provided in said act.

——— ———, *District Clerk of District No.* ———,
——— *County, N. J.*

NOTE.—In the cities the above notice is to be sent, by some person designated by the Board of Education, to the City Treasurer.

No. 73.—*Duties of Township Collector.*

1. To notify the County Superintendent of the amount of township school tax ordered, and the amount of interest on surplus revenue. [*Form* 18.]

2. To collect all township and district school taxes.

3. To receive and hold in trust all school moneys, and to pay out the same only upon orders drawn in accordance with forms 11 and 12.

4. To keep, in a book prepared for the purpose, an account with each School District. [*Form* 37.]

5. To make settlement with the Township Committee. [*Form* 20.]

6. To transmit copies of the settlement made with the Township Committee to the County Superintendent and to the Clerk of the Township. [*Form* 20.]

No. 74.—*Duties of District Clerk.*

1. To prepare and to post
   Notices for annual district meeting, [*Form* 49.]
   Notices for special district meeting, [*Form* 50.]
   and Notices for Trustee election, [*Form* 44.]

2. To prepare and to deliver notices for meetings of the Board of Trustees. [*Form* 45.]

3. To act as Secretary of the Board of Trustees. [*Form* 67.]

4. To record, in a book provided for that purpose, all the proceedings of trustee meetings and district meetings. [*Forms Nos.* 66, 67, 69 *and* 70.]

5. To keep an account of the finances of the District in a manner similar to that shown in Form 37.

6. To pay out all moneys by issuing orders on the Township Collector. [*Forms* 11 *and* 12.]

7. To make a financial report
   To County Superintendent, [*Form* 13.]
   To Township Committee, [*Form* 14.]
   and To annual district meeting, [*Form* 15.]

8. To make a report of the doings of the Trustees for the year to the annual district meeting for the election of Trustees. [*Form* 16.]

9. To take the District census.

10. To prepare and to forward the annual report to the County Superintendent.

11. To notify County Superintendent and Township Assessor of the amount of district school tax ordered. [*Forms* 17 *and* 52.]

12. To notify County Superintendent of the election of Trustees. [*Form* 46.]

13. To report the non-attendance of children at school. [*Form* 72.]

14. To attend the meetings of the "Township Board of Trustees" when convened by the County Superintendent.

15. To superintend repairs of buildings; to buy fuel, crayons, and such other articles as the Trustees may direct.

16. To deliver to his successor all records and papers belonging to the District.

No. 75.—*Form of Contract between District and Teacher.*

It is hereby agreed between "The Trustees of School District No. ———, in the County of ———," and ———, a qualified teacher, possessing a license in full force and effect, that the said ——— is to teach the public school of said District for a term [*here insert the time*], for the sum of ——— dollars per month, commencing on the ——— day of ———, 18——, and for such services, properly rendered, the said Trustees are to pay the said ——— monthly, the amount that may be due, according to this contract.

Dated this ——— day of ———, 18——.

——— ———, }
——— ———, } *Trustees of School District No. ———, in the County of ———.*
——— ———, }

——— ———, *Teacher.*

NOTE.—In case the Teacher is employed in a Graded School, the particular department for which he is engaged should be specified in the contract.

No. 76.—*Form of a Lease.*

Know all men by these presents, that A. B., of the Township of ———, in the County of ———, in the State of New Jersey, of the first part, for the consideration herein mentioned, does hereby lease unto "The Trustees of School District No. ———, in the County of ———," in the State aforesaid, party of the second part, and their assigns, the following described parcel of land:

[*here insert description of land.*]

Together with all the privileges and appurtenances thereunto belonging: To have and to hold the same for and during the term of ——— years from the ——— day of ———, A. D. 18——; and the said party of the second part, for themselves and assigns, do covenant and agree to pay the said party of the first part, for said premises, the annual rent of ——— dollars.

In testimony whereof, the said parties have hereunto set their hands and seals, this ——— day of ———, 18——.

A. B., *Lessor.*

C. D., }
E. F., } *Trustees of School District No. ———, in the County of ———, State of New Jersey.*
G. H., }

No. 77.—*Form of a Deed of a School House Site.*

Know all men by these presents, that A. B., [*and C. B., his wife, if married,*] in the Township of ———, in the County of ———, in the State of New Jersey, party of the first part, for and in consideration of the sum of ——— dollars, to them in hand paid by "The Trustees of School District No. ———, in the County of ———," and State aforesaid, party of the second part, the receipt whereof is hereby acknowledged, do hereby grant, bargain, sell, and convey to the said party of the second part, and their assigns, the following described piece of land, namely:

[*here insert description of land.*]

Together with all the privileges and appurtenances thereunto belonging: To have and to hold the same to the said party of the second part, and their assigns forever; and the said party of the first part, for themselves, their heirs, executors and administrators, do covenant, bargain and agree, to and with the said party of the second part, and their assigns, that at the time of the ensealing and delivery of these presents, they are well seized of the premises above conveyed, as of a good, sure, perfect, absolute and indefeasible estate of inheritance in the law in fee simple, and that the said lands and premises are free from all incumbrances whatsoever; and that the above bargained premises, in the quiet and peaceable possession of the said party of the second part and their assigns, against all and every person or persons lawfully claiming or to claim, the whole or any part thereof, the said party of the first part will forever warrant and defend.

In witness whereof, the said A. B. and C. B., his wife, party of the first part, have hereunto set their hands and seals, this ——— day of ———, A. D. 18——.

SIGNED, SEALED AND DELIVERED IN PRESENCE OF
E. F.

A. B. [SEAL.]
C. B. [SEAL.]

NOTE.—Such deed should be duly acknowledged before a judge, commissioner of deeds, master in chancery, or other officer authorized by law to take such acknowledgment, and recorded in the office of the County Clerk. The bond and mortgage given by the Trustees to secure payment of part of purchase money may be in the usual forms, and for the execution of deeds, mortgages and bonds, each District should have a corporate seal. Notes given for borrowed money should be in the name of the District and signed by all the Trustees as such.

No. 78.—*Form of Contract for Building a School House.*

Contract made and entered into between A. B., of the County of ———, State of New Jersey, and "The Trustees of School District No. ——, in the County of ———," State of New Jersey.

In consideration of the sum of one dollar in hand paid, the receipt whereof is hereby acknowledged, and of the further sum of ——— dollars, to be paid as hereinafter specified, the said A. B. agrees to build a frame school house and to furnish the materials therefor, according to the plan and specifications for the erection of said house hereto appended, at such point in said District as the said Trustees may designate. The said house is to be built of the best material, in a substantial, workmanlike manner; and is to be completed and delivered to said Trustees, or their successors in office, free from any lien for work done or materials furnished, by the ——— day of ———, 18——; and in case the said house is not finished in the time herein specified, the said A. B. shall forfeit and pay to the said Trustees, or their successors in office, for the use of said District, the sum of ——— dollars, and shall also be liable for all damages that may result to said District in consequence of such failure, and said Trustees may finish the building and charge the cost of the same to the said A. B.

The said Trustees, or their successors in office, in behalf of said District, hereby agree to pay the said A. B. the sum of ——— dollars when the foundation of said house is finished; and the further sum of ——— dollars when the building is ready for the roof; and the remaining sum of ——— dollars when the said house is finished and delivered, as herein stipulated.

It is further agreed that this contract shall not be sub-let, transferred or assigned, without the consent of both parties.

Witness our hands this ——— day of ———, 18——.

A. B., *Contractor,*

C. D., E. F. and G. H., *Trustees.*

NOTE.—In building a school house, it is all important to secure a plan of the building, with full specifications as to its dimensions, style of architecture, number and size of the windows and doors, quality of the materials to be used; what kind of roof; number of coats of paint; of what material the foundation shall be constructed; its depth below, and its height above the surface of the ground; the number and style of chimneys and flues; the provisions for ventilation; the number of coats of plastering and style of finish, and all other items in detail that may be deemed necessary. The plan and specifications should be attached to the contract, and the whole filed with the District Clerk. Before the building is commenced, the contract should be filed in the office of the County Clerk to prevent liens.

No. 79.—*Bond to be Issued for Loan from School Fund.*

No. ——. Bonds of School District No. ——. $———.

——— County, N. J.

Know all men by these presents, that "The Trustees of School District No. ——, in the County of ———," in the State of New Jersey, are justly indebted unto ——— ———, or bearer, in the sum of ——— dollars, lawful money of the United States of America, to be paid to the said ——— ———, or bearer, on the ——— day of ———, 18——, at the ——— Bank, ———, N. J., with interest therefor from the date hereof, at the rate of six per cent. per annum, payable semi-annually, on the ——— days of ——— and ——— in every year, at the bank aforesaid, on the presentation of the annexed coupons, as they severally become due.

This is one of a series of coupon bonds of ——— dollars each, issued by the Trustees of said School District, amounting in the aggregate to —— dollars, numbered from —— to ——, both inclusive; and the said bonds are issued for money borrowed by said Trustees for the purpose of building a school house in said School District, pursuant to the statute entitled "An Act to Establish a System of Public Instruction," approved March 27th, 1874, and by the consent of the inhabitants of said District lawfully given, at a meeting lawfully held on ———, 18——.

In witness whereof, on the ——— day of ———, in the year eighteen hundred and ———, this bond is signed by the Trustees of said District, and attested by the Clerk, under the seal of said District.

——— ———,

——— ———,

——— ———,

Attest ——— ———, *District Clerk.* *Trustees.*

[*Form of Coupon to be attached to the above Bond.*]

School District No. ——, County of ———, N. J.

SCHOOL HOUSE LOAN.

Interest warrant for ——— dollars, payable at the ——— Bank, ———, N. J., to bearer, ——— ———, for six months' interest on Bond No. ——.

——— ———, *D. C.*

No. 80.—*Application for Loan from School Fund.*

To "The Trustees for the Support of Public Schools," of the State of New Jersey:

The "Trustees of School District Number ———, in the County of ———," in the State of New Jersey, ask to borrow of "The Trustees for the support of Public Schools," the sum of ——— dollars, for the purpose of building a school house in the aforesaid District; and offer as security for said loan the coupon bonds of said District, to the amount, at par, of said loan. Said loan and bonds were authorized by the inhabitants of said District when met, upon due and legal notice for that purpose, on the Tuesday of the week following the annual town meeting, in the Township in which said District is situate, in the year one thousand eight hundred and eighty ———. The principal of said loan is to be repaid in instalments of ——— dollars a year; the first instalment to be paid on the ——— day of ———, one thousand eight hundred and eighty ———, and then yearly thereafter, with interest from date, at the rate of six per centum, according to the terms aforesaid. Principal and interest payable at ———; and the bonds hereby offered are of the denomination of $——— each, and are numbered from one to ——— both inclusive.

We submit herewith a copy of the proceedings had at said meeting of said inhabitants, duly verified; and a copy of the notice of said meeting, with an affidavit showing when and where said notice was put up.

Dated ———, ———, N. J., ——— ———, 18———.

——— ———, *D. C.* } *Trustees of School District*
——— ———, } *Number* ———, *in the*
——— ———, } *County of* ———, *N. J.*

NOTE.—The above application should be sent to the Secretary of State, who is ex officio Secretary of the Board of Trustees.

No. 81.—*Directions given to Candidates for Certificates before being Examined.*

1. Write your name and the subject of the examination, distinctly, at the top of each page.

2. You need not copy the questions upon the paper, but be careful to number each answer to correspond with the question.

3. Write only on one side of the paper, and do not write to the left of the red marginal line.

4. If unable to answer any question, write its proper number, and opposite the same write, "I cannot answer."

5. In answering questions in Arithmetic, Algebra, etc., give the work as well as the answer.

6. After beginning a set of questions, do not leave the room without the permission of the examiner in charge, until that exercise is completed.

7. During the examination, avoid, with the utmost strictness, all communication with other candidates, with visitors, or with any one else, except the examiners, whether by talking, signs, notes or otherwise. Any violation of this rule will cause your exercise to be rejected.

8. Referring to text books, or to written or printed abstracts, or memoranda of any kind connected with the subject of examination, or having such book, abstract or memoranda in your desk or about your person, will cause your exercise to be rejected.

9. As soon as one exercise is finished, hand it to the examiner in attendance before beginning another.

10. Do not fold the paper containing your answers, and do not tear off any portion of the sheet that may remain after you have finished a set of questions, but leave the sheet whole, as the paper will be preserved.

11. A special average will be given for correctness in Orthography and Composition, and for legibility, order, neatness and general appearance of the examination papers.

12. Be careful to preserve this card of directions and the questions. They will both be called for at the close of the examination.

No. 82.—*Calendar for School Elections and Duties.*

1. *State Board of Education*—Meets on the first Thursdays of February and November, and on the last Thursday of June, annually.

2. *Trustees of the School Fund*—Meet on the first Monday in April, annually, and at other times when called together by the Governor.

3. *State Board of Examiners*—Meets on the Mondays preceding the first Thursday of February and the last Thursday of June, annually.

4. *County Boards of Examiners*—Meet on the last Saturday of February, May, November, and the last Friday of August, annually.

5. *State Association of School Superintendents*—Meets at the call of the State Superintendent.

6. *School Trustees*—Elected on the first day of July, annually, except when the first falls on Sunday, when the election is held on the second day of July, and should meet on the first Tuesday after the first Monday in March, June, September and December, and oftener if necessary.

7. *District Clerks*—Elected within ten days after the annual meeting for the election of Trustees, annually.

8. *Township Boards of Trustees*—Meet semi-annually, at such times and places as the County Superintendent may appoint.

9. *District Meetings for Voting District Tax*—Held on the Tuesday of the week following town meeting, annually, or at the call of the Trustees.

10. *Report of the State Board of Education to the Governor*—On or before the tenth of November, annually.

11. *Report of the State Superintendent to the State Board of Education*—On the first Thursday in November, annually.

12. *Report of County Superintendents to the State Superintendent*—On or before the first of October, annually.

13. *Report of District Clerks to County Superintendent*—On or before the first of September, annually.

14. *Report of Teachers to Trustees*—At the close of each quarter's teaching.

15. *Monthly Reports by County Superintendents*—To the State Superintendent on the first Monday of each month.

16. *Financial Statement of Township Collector to Township Committee and County Superintendent*—On or before the first of September, annually.

17. *Financial Statement of District Clerks to Township Committee*—On or before the first of September, annually.

18. *Financial Statement of District Clerks to the County Superintendent*—On or before the first of September, annually.

19. *Assessor makes Returns to the Collector*—Within fifteen days after the first Monday in September, annually.

20. *Township and District School Taxes*—Collected and due the Trustees by the first of December, annually.

21. *District Census*—Taken between the first and the twentieth days of August, annually.

22. *Apportionment of State Appropriation to the Counties*—Made by the State Superintendent, on or before the first Monday in April, annually.

23. *Apportionment of State Appropriation and Township School Taxes to the Districts*—Made by the County Superintendent on or before the first of May, annually.

24. *Copy of Apportionment*—Made by the County Superintendent, and furnished to each Township Collector and District Clerk within twenty days after the apportionment is made.

25. *State Appropriation*—One hundred thousand dollars paid in November, and the State school tax in the month of January following.

26. *Visitation of Schools*—Each school visited by the County Superintendent twice every year.

27. *Agricultural College*—Candidates examined by the County Superintendents at the quarterly examination on the last Friday in August, annually.

28. *School Holidays*—Christmas day, first day of January, fourth day of July, and such days of fasting or thanksgiving as may be appointed by the President of the United States, or by the Governor of this State.

29. *School Year*—Commences on the first of September, and ends on the thirty-first day of August.

30. *Fiscal Year*—The school fiscal year of the State coincides with the school year.

RULES AND REGULATIONS

FOR THE

Government of School Officers.

Prescribed by the State Board of Education in conformity with the act entitled "An act to establish a system of Public Instruction" (Sec. 2, Clause 1).

I.—COUNTY BOARD OF EXAMINERS.

1. The County Superintendent, together with those whom he may appoint as County Examiners, will hold four stated meetings for the examination of teachers during each year, in such places in the county as are most convenient of access to the teachers. The first examination will be held on the last Saturday in February; the second on the last Saturday in May; the third on the last Friday in August; and the fourth on the last Saturday in November.

2. He will issue certificates of three grades, to be called, respectively, First, Second and Third Grade County Certificates.

3. Candidates for the *Third Grade County Certificate* are to be not less than sixteen years old. No experience in teaching will be required. Applicants for a Third Grade Certificate will be examined in Orthography, Reading, Writing, Geography, Practical Arithmetic and English Grammar. The license will continue in force for one year from date.

4. Candidates for the *Second Grade County Certificate* are to be not less than seventeen years old, with an experience in teaching of not less than one year. The examination will be the same as that for the Third Grade Certificate, with the addition of the History of the United States, Book-keeping, and Theory and Practice of Teaching. The license will continue in force for three years from date.

5. Candidates for the *First Grade County Certificate* are to be not less than eighteen years old, with an experience in teaching of not less than two years. The examination will be the same as that for the Second Grade Certificate, with the addition of Physiology, Natural Philosophy, English Composition, Algebra, the Constitution of the United States, and the School Law of New Jersey. The license will remain in force for five years from date.

6. Applicants for employment as special teachers to give instruction in any of the subjects not prescribed in the certificates granted by the State or County Boards of Examiners, may be examined by the Board of Examiners in such subjects, who, when satisfied of their fitness to teach in any of the branches referred to, may issue special certificates to said applicants. Such certificates shall remain in force three years.

7. A new set of questions will be prepared for each County Examination, under the direction of the State Superintendent, and ten questions will be given in each study.

II.—STATE BOARD OF EXAMINERS.

8. The State Board of Examiners consists of the State Superintendent of Public Instruction and the Principal of the State Normal School.

9. This Board will grant certificates of three grades, to be called respectively, First, Second and Third Grade State Certificates, the third or lowest grade ranking one degree above the highest grade issued by County Board of Examiners.

10. Candidates for the *Third Grade State Certificate* are to be not less than nineteen years old. They will be examined in the following branches, to wit: Spelling, Reading, Penmanship, Book-keeping, Geography, English Grammar, Arithmetic, Algebra, Geometry, Trigonometry, History and Constitution of the United States, Natural Philosophy, Chemistry, Geology, Botany, Physiology, Theory and Practice of Teaching, and the School Law of New Jersey. The license will remain in force for seven years from date.

11. Candidates for the *Second Grade State Certificate* are to be not less than twenty-one years of age, with an experience in teaching of not less than two years. The examination will be the same as

that required for a Third Grade Certificate. The license will remain in force for ten years from date.

12. Candidates for the *First Grade State Certificate* are to be not less than twenty-five years old, with an experience in teaching of not less than four years. The examination will be the same as that required for the Second or Third Grade Certificate, with the addition of any two of the following works that each candidate may choose, namely: Hart's In the School Room, Well's Graded Schools, Abbott's Teacher, Barnard's American Pedagogy, Barnard's American Normal Schools, Herbert Spencer's Education, Wickersham's Methods of Instruction, Wickersham's School Economy, Russel's Normal Training, Jewell's School Government, Emerson and Potter's School and Schoolmaster, Sheldon's Elementary Instruction, Ogden's Science of Teaching, Northend's Teacher's Assistant, Northend's Teacher and Parent, Sewell's Principles of Education, and Burton's Culture of the Observing Faculties. Each candidate will be required to draw up a plan for organizing the schools of some large city. The license will be good for life.

13. All teachers who, in the judgment of the State Board of Examiners, and of the local School Superintendent, have been successful principals of a graded school or schools of several grades, or of a city high school, for a period of ten years or more, shall receive a First Grade State Certificate without examination.*

III.—GENERAL INSTRUCTIONS RELATING TO BOTH COUNTY AND STATE CERTIFICATES.

14. With the exception of Reading, Vocal and Instrumental Music, Elocution, Drawing and School Gymnastics, all examinations are to be conducted in writing.

15. Upon each County Teacher's Certificate will be written the special average in each study and the general average, each marked as a percentage upon the scale of 100.

16. A special average will be given for correctness in Orthography and Composition, and for neatness, order and general appearance of the Examination Papers.

17. Special credit marks will be allowed for ability to teach Music, Drawing, Elocution and School Gymnastics.

*By graded school is meant one having not less than five grades in charge of five teachers.

18. No license will be granted to a teacher whose general average falls below 70, or whose special average in any one of the studies required for the Third Grade County Certificate shall be less than 70.

19. All candidates are required to furnish testimonials from School Trustees or other responsible persons, as to their moral character, and as to the time and place in which they have taught, and their success therein.

20. The Second and Third Grade County Certificates will be good only for the County in which they are issued. The First Grade County Certificates, and all State Certificates, will be good for all parts of the State.

21. All certificates will be liable to be revoked for cause.

IV.—COUNTY SUPERINTENDENTS.

22. It shall be the duty of each County Superintendent to visit every school in his County at least twice in each year, and oftener if practicable.

23. He shall note at such visits, in a book provided for the purpose, to be designated "The Superintendent's Visiting Book," the condition of the school buildings and out-houses, the appearance and correctness of the records kept in the School Registers, the efficiency of the teachers, the character, record and standing of the pupils, the methods of instruction, the branches taught, the text books used, and the discipline, government, and general condition of each school; and from the notes thus taken he shall ascertain and report the relative grade of merit of each school.

24. He shall give such directions in the science, art, and methods of teaching, as he may deem expedient, and shall be the official adviser and constant assistant of the school officers of his county. (School Law, Sec. 28.)

25. He shall distribute promptly all reports, forms, laws, circulars and instructions which he may receive from, and in accordance with the directions of the State Superintendent.

26. He shall take care that the decisions of the State Superintendent, or of the State Board of Education, upon controversies relating to the school laws of the State, or to the rules and regulations prescribed by the State Board of Education, be complied with

by the parties concerned; and in case such decisions are not complied with, he shall inform the State Superintendent thereof, and state the circumstances connected therewith. (School Law, Sec. 28.)

27. He shall carefully preserve all reports of school officers and teachers, and all the examination papers of teachers examined by the County Board of Examiners, and, generally, shall carry out the provisions of the law "Establishing a System of Public Instruction," and the rules and regulations prescribed by the State Board of Education, and at the close of his official term shall deliver to his successor all records, books, documents, papers, and property belonging to the office.

28. No County Superintendent shall act as agent for any author, publisher or bookseller, nor directly or indirectly receive any gift, emolument, or reward for his influence in recommending or procuring the use of any book, or school apparatus, or furniture of any kind whatever, in any public school; and any one who shall violate this provision shall be subject to removal from office.

29. He shall meet each Township Board of Trustees at least twice each year, which meetings shall be held at such times and places as he may appoint. (School Law, Sec. 31*a*, 40.)

30. He shall ascertain from the Township Collectors, within five days after the annual town meetings, the amount of school tax ordered to be assessed in each Township, and on or before the first day of May of each year he shall apportion, according to law, to the several Townships and School Districts of his County, all the school moneys to which they are entitled for the following year, whether received by State appropriation or ordered to be assessed as township school tax. (School Law, Sec. 23.)

31. He shall encourage and assist in the organization and management of County Institutes, and labor in every practicable way to elevate the standard of teaching and improve the condition of the public schools in his County; he, together with the City Superintendents, if any, of the cities within his County, shall organize annually a Teacher's Institute in the County, the time and place for holding the Institute, the instructors, and programme of exercises for the same, shall be such as the County and City Superintendents may agree upon, and as the State Superintendent may approve.

32. He shall inquire and ascertain whether the boundaries of the School Districts in his County are definitely and plainly described,

and shall keep in his office a full and correct transcript of such boundaries, a map of which he shall furnish to the State Superintendent of Public Instruction; in case the boundaries of any of the School Districts are conflicting or incorrectly described, or for any good reasons should be changed, he shall, upon consultation with the Trustees of the Districts concerned, harmonize, describe and change them, and make a report of such action to the State Board of Education; and on being ratified by said Board, the boundaries and descriptions so made shall be the legal boundaries and descriptions of the Districts of the County. (Sec. 24.) After the boundaries of the Districts of any County shall have been definitely determined by the action of the County Superintendent and the State Board of Education, the County Superintendent shall proceed to renumber them from number one to a number equal to the number of Districts in the County, inclusive; and no further changes shall be made unless the consent of the State Board of Education shall have been first obtained, as is herein provided. (School Law, Sec. 38.)

33. No contract between a Board of Trustees and a teacher shall at any time be made which will be binding upon a succeeding Board for a longer period than three months.

34. No changes in the boundaries of Districts, in which District taxes have been ordered, shall be made between the times of ordering and assessing the same.

35. Each County Superintendent shall, upon the first Monday in each month, send to the State Superintendent a brief report respecting the condition and progress of education in his County, and the work he has performed in connection with the duties of his office.

36. At the close of their official terms, or on the vacation of their office, by resignation or otherwise, should the same occur during the scholastic year, all County Superintendents shall report to the State Superintendent for the portion of the year that may have expired, as provided for in the 30th Section of the School Law, with reference to their annual reports; and no order shall be given for their last quarter's salary until such reports are received in a manner satisfactory to the State Superintendent.

37. That in case of the failure of any County Superintendent to make his report to the State Superintendent on the first day of September, as required by law, the State Superintendent shall not give to such County Superintendent any order for the payment of salary

for the quarter next succeeding such delinquency, except by a special resolution of the State Board of Education for this purpose.

38. All changes made in the boundaries of School Districts, against which no appeals are made in writing, may be approved by the State Superintendent, as Secretary of the State Board.

39. County Superintendents, on granting certificates at private examinations, may grant them in the usual form; or, if they deem it advisable, they may grant them to be good only until the regular quarterly examination next succeeding such private examination.

40. All teachers are required to attend the annual Institute held in the County in which they are teaching, except for cause satisfactory to the County Superintendent, and no deduction shall be made by Trustees from the salary of teachers for the time they are in actual attendance upon said Institute.

41. No teacher shall be employed by a Board of Trustees except such as hold regular teachers' certificates in full force and effect at the time the engagement is made.

42. The terms of the County Superintendents, heretofore and hereafter appointed, shall terminate with the School Year.

43. When it is within the knowledge of the State Superintendent that a County Superintendent is not attending to the duties of his office, he shall withhold from such County Superintendent orders for his quarterly salary until the Board shall direct such orders to be drawn.

44. Normal graduates, who have completed the two years' course, shall be entitled to the Third Grade State Certificate, and those who have completed the three years' course shall be entitled to the Second Grade State Certificate.

INDEX.

INDEX.

THE SCHOOL LAW.

BLANKS AND FORMS.

FORMS FOR DISTRICT CLERK—*Continued.* Page.

FORMS FOR DISTRICT TRUSTEES.

AN ACT concerning cities of the third class.

1. BE IT ENACTED *by the Senate and General Assembly of the State of New Jersey,* That in cities of the third class the term of office of members of the board of education shall be for as many years as there are members of such board of education elected from each ward; and that at each annual municipal election after the next succeeding election, each ward shall elect one member of such board of education.

2. *And be it enacted,* That at the next succeeding municipal election the members of the board of education shall be elected as heretofore, and at the first meeting of such board of education then elected, the members from each ward shall, by lot, divide themselves into classes, so that the term of office of one member from each ward shall expire in each succeeding year.

3. *And be it enacted,* That this act shall take effect immediately.

Approved February 20, 1883.

SUPPLEMENT to an act entitled "An act concerning taxes," approved April fourteenth, one thousand eight hundred and forty-six.

1. BE IT ENACTED *by the Senate and General Assembly of the State of New Jersey,* That hereafter there shall not be assessed upon any inhabitant of this state any poll tax for any of the purposes provided for in any special or local law of this state in excess of the sum of one dollar, any such special or local law or any general law of this state to the contrary notwithstanding.

2. *And be it enacted,* That in all the counties in this state where any special or local law now provides for the assessment of a poll tax in excess of the sum of one

dollar for any purpose whatever, the tax necessary for such purpose shall hereafter be assessed and levied upon the property in such county in the same manner as other counties are now assessed and levied.

3. *And be it enacted,* That all acts and parts of acts inconsistent with this act are hereby repealed, and this act shall take effect immediately.

Approved March 5, 1883.

AN ACT to limit the age and employment hours of labor of children, minors and women, and to appoint an inspector for the enforcement of the same.

1. BE IT ENACTED *by the Senate and General Assembly of the State of New Jersey,* That after the fourth day of July, one thousand eight hundred and eighty-three, no boy under the age of twelve years, nor any girl under fourteen years of age, shall be employed in any factory, workshop, mine, or establishment where the manufacture of any goods whatever is carried on.

2. *And be it enacted,* That on and after the first day of July, one thousand eight hundred and eighty-four, no child between the ages of twelve and fifteen years shall be employed in any factory, workshop, mine, or establishment where the manufacture of any kinds of goods whatever is carried on, unless such child shall have attended, within twelve months immediately preceding such employment, some public day or night school, or some well recognized private school; such attendance to be for five days or evenings every week during a period of at least twelve consecutive weeks, which may be divided into two terms of six consecutive weeks each, so far as the arrangement of school terms will permit, and unless such child, or his parents or guardian shall have presented to the manufacturer, merchant, or other em-

ployer seeking to employ such child, a certificate giving the name of his parents or guardian, the name and number of the schools attended, and the number of weeks in attendance, such certificate to be signed by the teacher or teachers of such child; *provided*, that in case the age of the child be not known, such teacher shall certify that the age given is the true age, to the best of his or her knowledge and belief; *provided*, that in case of orphan children, where necessity may seem to require, the guardian or others having charge of the same may, upon application to the inspector provided for in this act, receive from him a permit for the employment of such child or children, under such regulations as the said inspector may prescribe.

3. *And be it enacted*, That no child or children under the age of fourteen years shall be employed in any factory, workshop, mill, or establishment where the manufacture of any kind of goods is carried on, for a longer period than an average of ten hours in a day, or sixty hours in a week.

4. *And be it enacted*, That every manufacturer, merchant, or other employer employing any person contrary to the provisions of this act, or who shall be guilty of any violation hereof, shall be guilty of a misdemeanor, and upon conviction be fined for each offence, in a sum of not less than fifty nor more than one hundred dollars, and in default of payment of the same, shall be imprisoned in the county jail for not less than thirty nor more than ninety days, and that every head of a family, parent or guardian, who knowingly permits the employment of such children shall be likewise subject to a fine of not more than twenty-five nor less than ten dollars, for every child so employed, and for each offence, and in default of such payment, shall be imprisoned in the county jail for a period of not less than ten days nor more than twenty days; a certificate of the age of the minor, made by him or her, and by his or her parent or guardian, at the time of employment, shall be conclusive evidence of

the age of such minor, upon any trial for the violation of this act; *provided*, that the provisions in this act, in relation to the hours of employment, shall not apply to or affect any person engaged in preserving perishable goods in fruit-canning establishments.

5. *And be it enacted*, That the governor shall, immediately after the passage of this bill, appoint, with the advice and consent of the senate, some suitable person, who shall be a resident and citizen of this state, as inspector, at a salary of twelve hundred dollars per year, to be paid monthly, whose term of office shall be for three years; the said inspector shall be empowered to visit and inspect, at all reasonable hours, and as often as practicable, the factories, workshops, mines and other establishments in the state where the manufacture or sale of any kind of goods is carried on, and to report to the governor of this state on or before the thirty-first day of October, in each year; it shall also be the duty of said inspector to enforce the provisions of this act, and prosecute all violations of the same in any recorders' courts of cities, and justices of the peace, or other courts of competent jurisdiction in the state.

6. *And be it enacted*, That all necessary expenses incurred by said inspector, in the discharge of his duty, shall be paid from the funds of the state, upon the presentation of proper vouchers of the same; *provided*, that not more than five hundred dollars shall be expended by him in any one year.

7. *And be it enacted*, That all fines collected under this act shall enure to the benefit of the school fund of the district where the offence has been committed.

8. *And be it enacted*, That all acts and parts of acts inconsistent with the provisions of this act are hereby repealed, and that this act shall take effect immediately.

Approved March 5, 1883.

Supplement approved March tenth, eighteen hundred and eighty-three.

AN ACT regulating the number of school trustees to be elected in the respective school districts of this state, being a supplement to an act entitled "An act to establish a system of public instruction," approved March seventeenth, one thousand eight hundred and seventy-four.

1. BE IT ENACTED, *by the Senate and General Assembly of the State of New Jersey,* That whenever it shall appear by the annual school census that there are five hundred (500) or more children of legal school age in any school district having but three trustees, then it shall be lawful for the legal voters of the said district at their next annual meeting for the election of school trustees, to determine by a majority vote of those present whether the number of school trustees shall or shall not be increased to six (6).

2. *And be it enacted,* That in case it be decided to increase the number of school trustees in any such school district to six, then the said legal voters shall proceed to elect in the manner in which school trustees are now elected, three additional trustees, one to hold office for one year, one for two years and one for three years, and annually thereafter trustees shall be elected for the terms of three years to fill the places of those whose terms expire.

3. *And be it enacted,* That in case it be decided not to increase the number of school trustees, the vote shall be binding upon the district for that year only.

4. *And be it enacted,* That it shall be the duty of the district clerk in districts coming within the provisions of the first section of this act, in his notices of the annual meetings for the election of school trustees, to insert a notice that there are within the district five hundred (500) or more children of legal school age, and

that it will be determined at said annual meeting whether the board of school trustees shall consist of three or six; *provided*, that in case it shall be determined at any such meeting not to increase the number to six, then the clerk of said district shall not again insert such notice unless directed so to do by a vote of the trustees; *provided further*, that no vote shall be taken upon this subject unless public notice shall have been given as herein provided for.

5. *And be it enacted*, That all acts or parts of acts inconsistent with the provisions of this act be and the same are hereby repealed.

6. *And be it enacted*, That this act shall take effect immediately.

Amendment passed March twenty-third, eighteen hundred and eighty-three.

1. Be it enacted *by the Senate and General Assembly of the State of New Jersey*, That section twenty-six of the act entitled "An act to establish a system of public instruction" [Revision], approved March twenty-seventh, one thousand eight hundred and seventy-four, be and the same is hereby amended so as to read as follows:

26. *And be it enacted*, That he shall have power to withhold that part of the state appropriation derived from the revenue of the state from any district in which the inhabitants fail to provide a suitable school building and outhouses; *provided*, that no building of two or more stories, used for the purpose of public instruction, in which any of the doors, at places of exit, are so constructed as to open inwardly, shall be considered a suitable school building within the meaning of this section.

www.ingramcontent.com/pod-product-compliance
Lightning Source LLC
Chambersburg PA
CBHW030615270326
41927CB00007B/1188
* 9 7 8 3 3 3 7 2 3 2 4 9 8 *